1

ISBN:979-8-9990779-5-0

This book is intended as a practical resource and informational guide. It is not a substitute for professional counseling or therapy. The author and publisher assume no liability for outcomes related to the use of this book.

The Shifu of Sherman Oaks
Presence, Stillness, and Endurance in the Modern World

by

Ethan Starke

This book is not written to impress.
It is written to endure.

To honor the stillness that precedes motion.
To teach without noise.
To build what outlasts the builder.

To those who build without applause.
And lead without losing themselves.

INTRODUCTION

The Shifu of Sherman Oaks

The world does not slow down.
It accelerates — louder, faster, heavier with noise.

Mastery is not found by escaping it.
It is found by standing inside it — unmoved.

At the Shaolin Temple in Sherman Oaks, surrounded by the city's
rush, I learned what the world cannot teach:
Stillness is not retreat.
It is foundation.
Motion is not frenzy.
It is discipline.

The Shifu is not hidden on a mountain.
He is here — among traffic, deadlines, and demands.
Moving without haste.
Leading without pride.
Building without noise.

Shaolin does not train you to withdraw from life.
It trains you to remain intact within it.

To act without rushing.
To speak without shouting.
To lead without losing yourself.

Stillness in motion.
Presence under pressure.
Strength without performance.

The Shifu of Sherman Oaks is not a title.
It is a way of living where no one expects mastery to exist —
among the ordinary chaos of the modern world.

Not apart from it.
Inside it.
Fully.

This book is not about retreat.
It is about endurance.
It is about presence in motion —
life lived quietly, deeply, fully — even here.

Chapter 1:

What Cannot Be Seen

True mastery begins where no one watches.

Mastery is not a crown to be worn. It is not earned in the echo of applause or in the reflection of other people's eyes. It begins where no one watches — in the silent rooms, in the unremarkable mornings, in the days that pass without witness.

The work that endures is the work done unseen. The hand that shapes slowly, privately, without craving recognition. In the absence of an audience, the craftsman meets himself. Stripped of praise, stripped of judgment, stripped of any mirror but the one he cannot escape — the mirror within.

There is a kind of freedom here, and also a kind of terror. Without others watching, there is no one to affirm, no one to blame, no one to entertain. Only the quiet question lingers: will you do the work anyway?

This is where most turn back. When the shine fades and the task remains. When the rewards are not immediate, and the growth is not visible, and the days feel endless and small. Without validation, the spirit is tested. Without audience, the intentions are purified.

True mastery begins not with ambition, but with devotion — devotion to the practice, devotion to the process, devotion to the invisible work that no one will ever applaud.

To sit in stillness for hours with no proof of progress. To move through forms with no one clapping at the end. To carry water, chop wood, breathe, sweat, endure — not because anyone will see it, but because it is the way.

The early mornings that no one records. The repetitions that no one counts. The failures that no one consoles. The small, steady choices that, alone and unnoticed, build something that cannot be taken away.

True mastery is not a performance. It is a private covenant, made and kept in the dark, long before the light arrives.

The invisible practice that outlasts public applause.

Applause is a shallow echo. It fills the moment, but it fades quickly. It is easy to chase — easier still to depend on. But anything built on applause is built on sand. It will not hold.

What outlasts the applause is what was done long before it, and what continues long after it is gone.

Invisible practice is different. It does not decorate the outside — it fortifies the inside. It carves slowly, not into reputation, but into character. Day after day, it sculpts a form no one can see, but everyone can feel. A quiet weight. A gravity. A presence.

You do not see the roots of a tree, but they are there, deep in the soil, anchoring the trunk against the storm. Without them, the height is meaningless. It is the same with mastery. The visible is supported by the invisible. The gesture by the discipline. The action by the practice.

Invisible practice does not bend to mood. It is not stirred by praise or silenced by neglect. It is carried out in heat and in cold, in light and in dark, without witness, without reward. It is a practice not of the hands alone, but of the heart.

And it is precisely this invisibility that gives it power. Because no one watches, the practice is pure. Because no one rewards it, the commitment is real. Because no one cares, the only one left to care is you.

Mastery that is only public is fragile. Mastery rooted in invisible practice cannot be undone. It becomes the way you move, the way you breathe, the way you respond when the world shifts and tests what you claim to be.

It outlasts the seasons. It outlasts the critics and the crowds. It outlasts the noise. It remains, steady and unseen, shaping the future quietly.

Invisible practice — not the ceremony of greatness, but its true seed.

Endurance without recognition.

Recognition is a sweet poison. It tastes good in the moment, but it weakens the will. It tempts you to work for the applause instead of the craft, to chase the light instead of the path. Over time, it erodes the endurance it pretends to reward.

To endure without recognition is to build something the world cannot touch. When there is no praise to gather, no attention to collect, the work becomes clean. It ceases to be a performance and returns to what it was always meant to be — a practice, a discipline, a way of being.

Endurance without recognition requires a deeper fuel. Ego will not sustain it. Pride will not sustain it. Only devotion will. Devotion to the path itself, to the slow and private labor of becoming.

The world will not clap for the early mornings you rise to train. It will not notice the hours you spend refining what no one will ever see. It will not offer awards for the moments you choose integrity over ease, silence over noise, substance over show.

But in these unseen moments, something is forged that recognition cannot give you: a heart that does not depend on the world to know its worth. A mind that does not tremble in the face of silence. A body that carries its discipline quietly, unshaken by the absence of applause.

To endure without recognition is to belong to the work itself, not to its rewards. It is to find joy in the practice, strength in the silence, freedom in the fact that nothing is owed to you and nothing is required of you except the next right step.

Recognition may come or it may not. It is irrelevant. The work endures. The endurance itself becomes the reward.

Strength is built in the unseen hours.

Strength is not built in the moment of display. It is not earned under the lights or in the brief flare of accomplishment. Strength is a slow accumulation — a silent architecture of effort, layered in hours no one counts and moments no one marks.

The unseen hours are quiet and thankless. There are no banners, no ceremonies. Only the repetition of the small, the difficult, the easily ignored. A step, a breath, a stance held longer than comfort allows. The mind protests. The body protests. But the practice continues.

These are the hours that do not show themselves until they are needed. When pressure comes, the body does not collapse — it remembers. When failure looms, the mind does not fracture — it steadies. Not because of a sudden miracle, but because of countless forgotten repetitions.

Strength is built when no one is watching, and more importantly, when you are tempted to believe it does not matter. It is built when the progress is invisible, when the work feels hollow, when doubt whispers that no one will ever see, and nothing will ever come of it.

But it is precisely in these moments that real strength grows — deep, quiet, unseen. It grows not as spectacle but as foundation, preparing you for days when the visible world demands proof of what the invisible world has forged.

The strong do not appear suddenly. They reveal the hours they have endured in silence. They reveal the structure built when no one else cared, when even they themselves questioned, but did not quit.

Strength built in the unseen hours is different. It is not brittle. It is not loud. It does not boast. It endures.

Mastery is a private covenant, made and kept in the dark.

Mastery is not a contract signed in public. It is a covenant made in silence, in darkness, in the private places where no audience is present and no witnesses are called.

It is made in the early hour when no one sees you rise. In the quiet room where no one hears you practice. In the long, unlit corridors of doubt where you continue forward without certainty, without reward, without promise.

This covenant is not a promise to the world — it is a promise to yourself. A vow not to achievement, but to becoming. Not to glory, but to the path.

It is forged in the decision to show up when there is no visible progress. To continue refining when no one is paying attention. To uphold standards no one is asking you to keep. To walk with discipline long after motivation has faded and ambition has grown quiet.

Mastery requires this hidden loyalty — not loyalty to the outcome, but to the process. To the daily, ordinary acts that stitch strength into the body and wisdom into the soul. To the invisible stitches that hold the visible together.

No one else can make this covenant for you. No one else can see if you keep it. It is not an oath made aloud. It is not written in ink. It is written in time — in days and years — and sealed not by applause, but by persistence.

And when, much later, the world calls it mastery, it will still be something they cannot see — only something they can sense. A weight in your movements. A clarity in your choices. A calm that does not shake.

Mastery is not performance. It is not decoration. It is a private covenant — made and kept in the dark — known only to those who have walked far enough without witnesses to know its worth.

Chapter 2:

Anchoring Before Acting

Stillness is the root — motion grows from it.

Action without stillness is like a river without a source. It may rush forward, but it has no clarity, no direction, no endurance. It exhausts itself quickly, spinning and scattering, lost before it truly begins.

Stillness is not the enemy of action — it is its origin. It is the root from which all true motion grows.

The world admires speed, prizes hustle, rewards those who move first and move loudest. But motion without anchor is drift, not journey. It is noise, not music.

Stillness is not merely the absence of movement; it is the quiet gathering of energy. It is the slow accumulation of direction, the silent alignment of will and purpose. It is the pause that sharpens the arrow before it flies, the breath that centers the body before it strikes.

In the quiet of stillness, you listen. Not to the noise of the world, but to the deeper currents within. You find not just what you want to do, but why you must do it. Not just where you wish to go, but who you must become to travel there.

Stillness clarifies. It reveals the unnecessary and the urgent, the false and the true. It strips away the distractions that disguise themselves as duties. It teaches you to move not because you are restless, but because you are ready.

And when the time for action comes, motion born from stillness carries a different weight. It is not frantic. It is not desperate. It does not flail or grasp. It moves with a quiet authority, a calm inevitability. It knows its root, and because it knows, it endures.

Without stillness, action burns out. With stillness, action becomes purpose made visible.

True movement is not forced. It grows, quietly and powerfully, from the deep soil of stillness.

Preparation is not delay — it is power.

In a world addicted to immediacy, preparation is misunderstood. It is seen as hesitation, as weakness, as fear of action. But real preparation is not delay — it is power gathered quietly, patiently, fully.

To prepare is not to avoid action. It is to ready yourself so completely that when the moment comes, action is natural, precise, and irreversible. It is to forge the mind until it no longer flinches, to train the body until it no longer doubts, to sharpen the spirit until it no longer hesitates.

Without preparation, action is thin and brittle. It may succeed for a moment, but it cannot endure. It cracks under pressure, folds under uncertainty, collapses when the stakes rise.

Preparation builds depth. It builds layers. It builds unseen reserves that can be drawn upon when the surface is tested. To prepare is to honor the difficulty ahead by refusing to meet it casually.

It is the unseen hours that steady the visible ones. The months of quiet practice that stabilize the single day of trial. The repetitions that no one records, the questions asked when no one listens, the doubts wrestled with in solitude.

A prepared mind moves differently. It does not rush; it advances. It does not flail; it strikes. A prepared heart beats steadily through chaos. A prepared body endures long after others fall.

Preparation is a quiet, patient form of love — love for the craft, for the path, for the life you are building. It is a refusal to offer the world anything less than what is worthy.

Delay is paralysis. Preparation is power. They may look the same to those who only glance. But they are not the same.

Delay comes from fear of movement.

Preparation comes from respect for movement.

And when the time comes to move, the one who has prepared will not need to rush. They will move like water released from a dam — inevitable, forceful, unhurried, unstoppable.

The world moves; the anchored remain unshaken.

The world is in constant motion. Tides rise and fall. Fortunes shift. Expectations press in from every side, urging movement, demanding response. It is easy to be caught in the current, to be dragged along by noise disguised as necessity.

But not all motion is progress. Not all reaction is wise. The world moves — endlessly, restlessly — but those who are anchored do not move with every wind. They are not shaken by each wave. They hold their ground, steady, deliberate, unseen beneath the surface but immovable in the deep.

To be anchored is not to be static. It is to move with intention, not compulsion. To act from choice, not from pressure. It is the deep root that allows the tree to bend without breaking, to withstand storms without being uprooted.

Without anchor, life becomes reaction — a life lived at the mercy of external forces. Every crisis pulls you. Every praise tempts you. Every fear directs you. You are no longer choosing your course; you are being chosen by the world's noise.

The anchored life is different. It listens carefully, moves cautiously, speaks slowly. It does not fear change, but it does not worship it either. It knows that change is inevitable, but direction is optional. It knows that storms pass, but roots remain.

Strength does not come from resistance to the storm. It comes from the quiet, invisible anchor beneath it. From the clarity that remains when confusion reigns. From the calm that remains when panic spreads.

In a world that moves without ceasing, it is easy to be caught up, to be tossed, to be lost. But the anchored remain. They may move, but they do not drift. They may change, but they do not lose themselves.

They endure, not because the world is gentle, but because they have rooted themselves deeper than the world can reach.

Chapter 3:
Living the Breath

Breath as life's quiet rhythm.

Breath is the first motion, the first rhythm. Long before we speak, before we walk, before we act, we breathe. Quiet, unseen, continuous — the breath moves through us, sustaining without announcing itself.

In breath, life offers its simplest lesson: motion and stillness are not separate. They are woven together, wave within wave, pulse within pulse. The inhale expands; the exhale releases. Tension, release. Energy, surrender. Motion, stillness. The breath does not ask permission. It simply is.

To live without awareness of breath is to live detached from the most basic rhythm of being. It is to hurry without pacing, to strain without release, to move without rest.

But to return to the breath is to return to life itself — not as concept, not as ambition, but as experience. Each inhale invites the world in. Each exhale surrenders to it. Breath teaches that receiving and letting go are not opposites; they are one motion, one necessity.

The world moves fast. Deadlines tighten. Demands pile. We forget to breathe — not just the physical act, but the deeper art of breathing: to meet life's movement with inner steadiness, to let the currents pass through without drowning in them.

The breath is patient. It waits for our return. It does not punish our forgetting. It simply continues, offering the chance, moment by moment, to begin again.

Those who live by the breath live by a different clock. Not the clock of urgency, but the clock of presence. They know when to hold and when to release, when to gather strength and when to soften.

In this rhythm, life unfolds more slowly, more clearly. The noise recedes. What matters returns. Breath by breath, the surface world loosens its grip, and the deeper life reemerges.

Breath — the quiet rhythm, the first teacher, the first return.

Effort and ease are not opposites — they are one current.

The mind, trained by the world, separates effort from ease. It calls one hard and the other soft, one worthy and the other indulgent. It tells us we must choose — push or relax, strive or surrender.

But the breath teaches differently.

Effort and ease are not rivals. They are partners in the same current, inseparable, flowing into and out of each other. Inhale —

effort. Exhale — ease. Work — release. Tension — surrender. Without one, the other collapses.

Effort without ease becomes rigidity. A body that cannot bend will break. A mind that cannot rest will shatter. A life that cannot soften will not endure.

Ease without effort becomes drift. A body that will not engage grows weak. A mind that refuses challenge grows dull. A life that avoids exertion becomes hollow.

But when effort and ease flow together, there is power. There is the tension of the bowstring — taut, but not brittle. There is the wave's rise and fall — strong, but never strained.

Shaolin practice reflects this unity. The stance is strong, but the breath within it is soft. The strike is sharp, but the mind behind it is calm. The training is rigorous, but it rests upon quietness, upon the disciplined return to center.

Living well is not a matter of choosing between striving and surrender. It is a matter of learning their dance — knowing when to push, when to yield, when to gather, when to release.

Effort and ease are not a conflict to be resolved. They are a current to be ridden. Like breath, like tide, like life.

Those who learn this rhythm move differently. They do not exhaust themselves fighting the world. They move with it, through it, because of it — carried not by force alone, but by flow.

Effort and ease, breath and release, motion and stillness — one current, one life.

The template of motion: internal calm, external flow.

In the stillness of breath, a deeper architecture reveals itself — a template not only for breathing, but for living, for moving, for being.

Internal calm. External flow.

This is the shape that breath models with every cycle, teaching without words. The body moves, but the center remains still. The chest rises and falls, but the heart stays steady. The air rushes in and out, but the mind stays clear, undisturbed by the movement it allows.

To live this way is to carry a kind of quiet into every action. It is to step forward without rushing, to lift burdens without strain, to speak without needing to be heard. The calm within does not resist the motion; it permits it, guides it, tempers it.

Most move with their storms on the outside and their turmoil on the inside. Their bodies push and pull, and their minds race faster still. But those who learn from breath carry the storm differently. The outer life may swirl, but the inner life remains a calm lake, reflecting, absorbing, unmoved.

This is not inaction. This is not detachment. It is engagement from a deeper place, action rooted in being rather than doing.

The warrior stands still inside his strike. The leader is quiet inside the noise. The creator is empty inside the moment of making, and thus full of it.

Internal calm does not prevent movement — it perfects it.
External flow does not scatter attention — it focuses it.

The breath reveals: motion is not the enemy of calm. Motion is its expression, its extension. True calm is not fragile. It moves through life without being undone by it.

To walk the world this way is to live aligned with the deepest currents, not against them. To move without losing oneself. To act without being unmade by action.

Breath by breath, life by life — internal calm, external flow.

Chapter 4:

Action Without Haste

Urgency is not mastery.

The world admires urgency. It rewards the fastest, the loudest, the first to move, the first to shout, the first to arrive. It mistakes motion for meaning, speed for strength.

But urgency is not mastery. Urgency is impulse dressed in ambition's clothes. It is the quick strike without the steady hand, the hurried decision without the measured heart.

Mastery does not move from urgency. It moves from clarity.

Urgency reacts. Mastery responds.

Urgency is frantic. It fears stillness, as if silence will steal its power. It rushes, not because it knows where to go, but because it fears being still long enough to see that it doesn't.

Mastery waits when it must. It acts when it should. It knows that not every motion is forward, not every step is progress, not every noise is truth. It trusts in timing deeper than the clock, and wisdom slower than the market.

Shaolin practice is deliberate. Every stance, every breath, every movement is placed with care. No rush. No scramble. No wasted energy. The Master does not race to strike; he waits until the strike is necessary — and when it comes, it is precise, final, unhurried.

To move without urgency is not to be passive. It is to reserve your strength until the moment demands it. It is to move so completely in alignment with necessity that the motion seems effortless.

Urgency burns fast and fades quickly. Mastery endures.

The one who hurries may arrive first, but the one who moves with purpose will arrive whole.

Speed without direction is erosion. Hurry without wisdom is exhaustion. Only deliberate action — rooted in patience, sharpened by clarity — can last beyond the initial surge of effort.

Urgency is not mastery. It is noise. Mastery is silence — moving when it is time to move, not before.

Power comes from deliberate pace.

Pace is not speed. Pace is not idleness. Pace is a rhythm — a chosen cadence that aligns action with intention, timing with clarity, movement with meaning.

The one who moves with deliberate pace moves with a power that urgency cannot match. It is not the power of acceleration, but the power of control. It is not the frantic energy of rushing to be first, but the focused energy of arriving when it matters.

Deliberate pace conserves energy where others waste it. It chooses direction before acceleration. It waits for the moment to mature before striking. Like a seasoned archer who holds the bowstring taut but waits, breath steady, heartbeat slow, for the precise instant when the shot is certain.

To move with deliberate pace is to resist the temptation to prove yourself quickly. It is to ignore the crowd's demand for spectacle and the inner demand for validation. It is to remember that the tallest trees grow slowly, that the deepest rivers flow steadily, that endurance is built not in bursts but in steady, patient persistence.

Shaolin forms are built on pace. Not the reckless energy of a beginner, but the measured progression of a practitioner who understands that form is more than appearance. It is breath matching movement, focus matching breath, purpose woven into each step.

Deliberate pace signals something rare: mastery over time. A refusal to be rushed by the fear of missing out, the fear of falling behind, the fear of being unseen. It is the mark of one who does not race time, but moves in harmony with it.

There is strength in knowing when not to move.

There is power in knowing that the fastest path is not always the one taken first.

Deliberate pace is not laziness; it is precision. It is knowing that great things are not built in haste. That deep roots are not planted in a season. That real power is patient — not because it must be, but because it can be.

The one who moves with deliberate pace does not waste their strike. They do not waste their life.

They move once. They move well.

The art of choosing when to move.

Not all moments are created equal. Some call for stillness. Some demand motion. The art is in knowing the difference — in feeling the subtle shift when the time is no longer for waiting, but for stepping forward.

Most do not choose when to move. They are moved — by pressure, by fear, by noise. They react to the loudest signal, the latest urgency, the first open door. They mistake availability for destiny, speed for necessity.

But the one who has learned to wait, to listen, to watch — this one moves differently. Their movement is not scattered; it is placed. It is not hurried; it is precise. Their steps are fewer, but heavier. Their actions are rarer, but deeper.

Choosing when to move is an art because it cannot be reduced to rules. It demands something deeper than strategy — it demands presence. A mind quiet enough to hear the change in the wind. A heart still enough to know when it is time to rise.

Shaolin teaches patience not as passivity, but as preparation. The Master waits not because he is unwilling to act, but because he knows that premature action is wasted strength. A strike thrown too early misses its mark. A mind moved too quickly misses its moment.

Timing is a form of intelligence — not just knowing what to do, but knowing when the world is ready to meet it.

The art of choosing when to move demands trust — trust in your own readiness, trust in the ripeness of the moment, trust that hesitation is not always cowardice, and that waiting is not always weakness.

It demands courage — to stay still when others rush, to hold ground when others scatter, to believe in the value of unseen preparation over the intoxication of early movement.

And when the moment finally comes — not when you are restless, not when you are desperate, but when the ground beneath you signals that it is time — the move is made.

Decisive. Precise. Without apology. Without regret.

True mastery is not just movement. It is the art of choosing when to move.

Chapter 5:

Motion Without Noise

Do not announce your every step.

In a world obsessed with visibility, the quiet path is radical. Everywhere, movement is paired with announcement, effort with exhibition. Every step taken must be displayed, every progress shared, every victory declared.

But real motion does not need noise. It moves without calling attention to itself. It builds without demanding witnesses.

The loud announce every small stride because they fear invisibility. They confuse being seen with being substantial. They crave the validation of an audience to confirm that their journey matters. But what is confirmed by others is not fortified within. Noise cannot make a shallow movement deep.

The quiet move differently. They step lightly, but their steps carve deeper paths. They do not announce every movement because they understand that noise dilutes force. Attention dispersed is energy lost.

The Shaolin strike is silent before it is swift. The master steps in stillness before stepping in speed. Movement is born in the silent preparation, not the shouted promise.

To move without announcing is not to hide. It is to protect the integrity of the motion. It is to preserve its power by refusing to fracture it across the opinions of others.

Noise seeks approval. Quiet seeks alignment.

When you announce every step, you give away the energy meant for movement. When you guard your steps in silence, the movement gathers force, gathering like a storm not yet revealed.

Those who move without noise arrive differently. They are not drained by needing to be seen. They are not weakened by needing to be praised. They move for the sake of the path itself — not for what it earns them.

To move without announcing is to remember: the river does not shout as it carves the canyon. It moves, it shapes, it endures — and when the work is done, the canyon remains.

Meaningful movement is quiet.

Noise is often mistaken for momentum. But the loudest motion is not always the deepest. In truth, the most meaningful movement rarely draws attention to itself. It does not announce, it does not boast, it does not insist.

It moves — quietly, steadily — like breath, like tide, like growth.

Meaningful movement does not demand recognition because it is not born for recognition. It is born from necessity. From a need rooted deeper than vanity — a need to build, to become, to answer a call not from the world, but from within.

Shaolin practice is built on such movement. The slow, deliberate repetition of form. The unremarkable stance held far beyond comfort. The breath drawn and released without fanfare. To the untrained eye, it seems simple. To the undisciplined heart, it seems unimpressive. But within that simplicity lies force, patience, clarity.

The greatest changes happen without spectacle. The seasons turn without applause. The mountains rise without announcement. The heart grows steady not in the light of recognition, but in the darkness of discipline.

When movement becomes noise, it loses its meaning. It becomes show, distraction, performance. It serves the eye, not the soul. It convinces others, but it convinces no one within.

Meaningful movement — the kind that builds lives, the kind that leaves real marks on the world — moves differently. It is quiet. It is slow to reveal itself. It is patient with its unfolding.

It does not need to be heard. It needs only to be done.

And because it does not scatter its force in shouting, it keeps its power intact. It grows unseen. It deepens silently. And when it arrives — when it emerges — it comes not as noise, but as inevitability.

The river does not announce its journey to the sea. It flows, and it arrives.

Motion that speaks without shouting.

There is a kind of movement that needs no introduction. It does not beg for attention. It does not shout its purpose. It moves — and by its movement alone, it speaks.

This kind of motion carries a different weight. It is not inflated by noise, but by substance. It does not impress by volume, but by clarity. It is felt before it is seen, understood before it is explained.

In Shaolin, the Master moves with this kind of gravity. Every step is deliberate. Every gesture complete. There is no wasted energy, no performance for the sake of onlookers. The movement itself carries meaning — not because it seeks to, but because it cannot help but do so.

Motion that speaks without shouting has its origin in stillness. It begins in the quiet understanding of why it moves at all. It is free from the hunger to be noticed. It carries no urgency to be celebrated. And because it carries none of this burden, it moves cleanly, directly, with force unobstructed by vanity.

You can see it in the way a craftsman handles their tools — no flourish, no performance, only the steady application of skill. You can hear it in the way a leader speaks — few words, each one placed with care, heavy with earned understanding. You can feel it in the way a warrior stands — calm, unshaken, not needing to prove what cannot be taken.

The world is full of shouting — gestures that say "look at me," movements designed to draw eyes but not to build anything lasting. But motion that speaks without shouting draws something deeper — not attention, but respect. Not applause, but trust.

It speaks through its integrity. It commands by its quietness. It endures because it does not scatter itself trying to be seen.

Noise fades quickly. True motion lingers — not in the ears, but in the bones.

Chapter 6:

The Weight of Intentionality

Every step carries consequence.

To move is not neutral. Every step shifts something. Every word shapes something. Every decision leaves a mark.

The world often speaks of action as if it were weightless, as if choices evaporate once made, as if consequences are rare exceptions instead of the natural shadow every act casts.

But every step carries consequence. Even the smallest. Even the unseen.

A word spoken in anger ripples beyond the moment. A decision made in haste sets chains of events into motion. A step taken without thought moves a life closer to chaos, even if the drift is slow and invisible at first.

In the practice halls of Shaolin, every movement is deliberate because every movement matters. A strike thrown carelessly is not merely ineffective — it is dangerous. A stance held poorly invites collapse, not just in posture but in principle.

So too in life. Careless action, reckless words, thoughtless steps — they all accumulate. Like drops of water carving stone, they shape the unseen foundation until one day the ground gives way.

Intentionality is not a burden. It is a recognition. A refusal to act as if what we do vanishes into nothingness.

To act with intentionality is to move knowing the weight of your motion, to speak knowing the reach of your words, to live knowing that your life leaves a trail — not always visible, but always real.

It demands something rare: presence before action, reflection before movement, awareness before impulse.

And it grants something even rarer: a life that is not spent undoing what has been done, a heart that is not heavy with unintended harm, a mind that does not tremble at the thought of its own wake.

Every step carries consequence. Those who remember this walk differently — slower, steadier, deeper. They do not scatter their steps in all directions. They do not wound carelessly. They move with the knowledge that life is not a stage for their movements, but a field where every step plants something that will grow, for good or ill.

The careless walk light. The wise walk heavy.

Intentional action outlasts chaotic energy.

Chaos burns bright. It moves quickly, loudly, furiously. It gathers attention because it is fire — sudden, wild, consuming.

But fire without direction leaves only ash. Motion without intention leaves only exhaustion. Energy spent in chaos vanishes. It is a burst — impressive in the moment, irrelevant afterward.

Intentional action is different. It does not rush to display itself. It does not explode; it builds. Quietly. Steadily. Unseen at first, and then undeniable.

In the beginning, chaotic energy looks more powerful. It flashes. It dazzles. It moves fast. But like all things without root, it cannot endure. The faster it burns, the faster it dies.

Intentional action outlasts because it is anchored. It draws not from the shallow wells of excitement, but from the deep reservoirs of clarity. It is not moved by urgency, but by necessity. It does not demand to be seen, because it is committed to being done.

In Shaolin, the forms are practiced not for performance but for permanence. They are built slowly into the body until they are no longer performance at all — they are presence. They do not decay under pressure. They do not scatter under scrutiny.

Intentional action is like this. It weaves into the fabric of life. It becomes the steady force that builds what is meant to last — not loudly, but fully.

The world often rewards chaotic energy. It chases the newest, the fastest, the loudest. But the world forgets quickly what it once applauded. Chaos is forgotten as easily as it is celebrated.

Intentional action lingers. It builds structures that do not crumble with the seasons. It shapes lives that do not unravel under pressure. It carves legacies that do not dissolve when the noise moves elsewhere.

To act intentionally is to move in a way that lasts. Not because it is loud, but because it is true.

Chaos exhausts. Intention endures.

Leadership is decided by what you choose to move.

Leadership is not the ability to move things — it is the wisdom to know which things to move.

The world is full of noise disguised as urgency, full of distractions disguised as duties. There are endless fires to chase, endless battles to fight. The leader who tries to move everything moves nothing well. The leader who tries to fix everything breaks himself.

Leadership is restraint before it is command. It is the discipline to let some fires burn. It is the clarity to know which rivers must be crossed and which must be allowed to run their course. It is the courage to remain still in the face of noise, to step only where steps matter.

Shaolin teaches this subtly. A master does not block every strike. He deflects the necessary ones. He does not counter every move. He counters the real threat. Every unnecessary motion is wasted energy — not just wasted, but dangerous, because it opens you to what truly matters.

Leadership moves the few things that need moving. It speaks the few words that need speaking. It shapes the few structures that need shaping. It is not paralyzed by the immensity of the world's noise because it has already decided what noise matters and what noise does not.

To lead is to move with intention, to move selectively, to move from principle, not panic. It is to understand that moving everything is not leadership — it is exhaustion. It is the wisdom to know that some things heal on their own, that some problems are not yours to solve, that some storms must be weathered, not fought.

The leader who moves intentionally does not burn out. He does not thrash against the inevitable. He moves only what must be moved — but when he moves, the whole landscape shifts.

He moves less, but his movement means more.

In a world where many move constantly and accomplish little, true leadership is decided not by how much you move, but by what you choose to move.

Chapter 7:

Craft Over Conquest

Skill before ambition.

Ambition is easy to ignite. It flares quickly — fueled by hunger, by dreams of conquest, by visions of achievement. But without skill beneath it, ambition burns shallow and dies early.

Skill before ambition — this is the old way, the slow way, the enduring way. It is the path not of the one who races to claim a prize, but of the one who prepares, silently, to deserve it.

Shaolin teaches this from the beginning. The student does not rush to spar before learning to stand. He does not seek victory before understanding form. He does not chase mastery before building the muscle of patience. First, he learns how to move — slowly, painfully, without recognition. Then he learns how to move well.

Only after long seasons of practice does ambition find its right place — not as the engine, but as the horizon.

Skill before ambition reverses the order the world encourages. It demands that you build before you brand, that you work before you proclaim, that you refine before you race.

The one who places ambition first often gains speed but loses direction. He moves fast but builds nothing he can stand on. His victories are hollow, easily undone by the first real test.

The one who places skill first moves slower — but deeper. He masters the craft before seeking the crown. And when the time for achievement comes, he is not fragile. He does not depend on luck or illusion. He stands on the foundation he has spent years building — stone by stone, breath by breath.

Skill humbles ambition. It tames it. It aligns it.

Without skill, ambition is blind. Without ambition, skill is stagnant. But when skill is placed first, ambition becomes not a wildfire, but a forge — shaping, directing, sustaining.

The deepest achievements do not come from those who chased the summit. They come from those who built the strength to carry themselves there — quietly, persistently, without announcement.

Skill before ambition. Always.

Shaolin practice: build as discipline, not dominance.

The world often mistakes building for conquest. It sees success as something seized, territory as something taken, achievement as a form of domination. But Shaolin practice teaches another way: build not to conquer, but to discipline. Build not to overpower, but to refine.

In Shaolin, strength is not for show, and victory is not for crushing others. Every form, every repetition, every breath is a gesture of discipline — an offering to the craft itself, not a weapon to wield over others.

The purpose is not to dominate the opponent, but to master the self.

The temple teaches: if you build only to conquer, you will build shallowly. Your strength will be a performance, hollow at the center, easily shattered when it meets something it cannot overwhelm.

But if you build to discipline yourself — if each motion is a vow to patience, to precision, to presence — then your strength becomes something else entirely. It is no longer a tool for victory alone; it is a foundation for endurance, for wisdom, for peace.

Discipline builds what dominance cannot: resilience without cruelty, power without arrogance, motion without vanity. It allows you to move without needing to be greater than another. It allows you to build without needing to prove yourself. It allows you to grow without needing to be seen.

In the end, the one who builds for dominance is always at war — with others, with the world, with himself. The one who builds for discipline finds something rarer: stillness within movement, mastery within humility, growth without end.

Building as discipline transforms the craft from a weapon into a way of life. It aligns action with intention, power with principle.

Dominance seeks to end the story — to finish, to win, to conquer. Discipline seeks to deepen it — to continue, to refine, to return.

The Shaolin way: build not to dominate, but to become.

Mastery expressed through creation.

True mastery does not declare itself in conquest. It reveals itself in creation.

The Master does not measure his strength by how many opponents he has defeated. He measures it by what he has built — within himself, within his craft, within the quiet spaces where no one is looking.

Creation is the truest sign of mastery because it demands more than force. It demands vision. It demands patience. It demands the discipline to shape something lasting out of raw, unformed potential.

In Shaolin, the greatest mark of training is not the ability to break, but the ability to make — to forge body and mind into tools for life, not just for combat. Every form is a kind of architecture, every breath a kind of scaffolding. Slowly, the student is not merely learning to fight; he is learning to build — a foundation of clarity, a structure of resilience, a home for enduring strength.

Creation requires more of us than conquest. It demands that we step beyond impulse. It requires that we not only take, but give. Not only dismantle, but assemble. Not only endure, but create something that endures beyond us.

Mastery is visible not in the battles won, but in the lives shaped, the structures built, the legacies left not in noise but in quiet presence.

The conqueror leaves behind ruins. The creator leaves behind roots.

To create is to extend yourself beyond the moment. It is to offer your strength not as dominance, but as offering — to the craft, to the world, to those who will come after you.

Those who master themselves build differently. They are not hurried by the market. They are not moved by trends. They do not seek to dazzle; they seek to endure. Their work grows slowly, layer by layer, unseen at first but unshakable when the storms come.

Mastery expressed through creation is different because it seeks not to dominate today, but to serve tomorrow.

In the end, the deepest mark of mastery is not what you have conquered — but what you have built.

Chapter 8:

Structures Built to Endure

Sacred architecture as model — built to outlast storms.

The ancients built differently. They built not for display, but for time. Not for the moment, but for the centuries that would follow. Sacred architecture was not made to impress those who walked past it once. It was made to withstand the storms, the wars, the decay of all things that time inevitably brings.

Stone was chosen not for its shine, but for its endurance. Foundations were laid not for speed, but for depth. Every joint, every seam, every hidden line of weight bore the quiet signature of those who understood that true creation is tested not by its beauty on the day it is made, but by its silence long after its makers are forgotten.

There is no hurry in a cathedral. There is no haste in a temple. These structures were built with time inside them. They were designed to carry the burden of years, to stand when lesser things fall.

Shaolin carries this understanding. The training is not a sprint toward strength, but a laying of invisible bricks — each stance, each breath, each repetition a stone in the foundation of a life meant to endure beyond the excitement of youth or the hunger for quick success.

To build what lasts, you must build differently. You must resist the modern temptation to rush. You must refuse the cheap materials of vanity and approval. You must lay foundations so deep they are invisible to others — but undeniable when the winds rise and the seasons change.

The structures that endure are rarely the ones that caught the most attention when they were new. They are the ones built quietly, patiently, with a hand steady enough to know that endurance is not given — it is built, piece by piece, in silence.

The world builds fast and watches it fall. But the sacred builders — those who care not just for now, but for what must stand when now is long gone — they build differently.

They build to endure.

Foundations deeper than appearances.

What the eye can see is always less important than what the eye cannot.

A foundation is unseen by design. Buried beneath the surface, it carries the weight of the structure without demanding attention for itself. It does not boast of its strength; it simply bears the burden.

The world, addicted to appearances, forgets this. It builds for the eye, for the instant impression. Gloss over grit. Shine over substance. Structures rise quickly, beautifully, impressively — but fall just as quickly when the storms come, because what lies beneath was neglected.

Endurance is invisible at first.

A house built for appearances will charm the passerby and betray the dweller. A life built for display will dazzle for a season and collapse when the ground shifts. Only what is anchored deeper than appearances can withstand the long weight of time.

Shaolin practice honors the foundation. Hours spent in silence. Forms repeated with no audience. Muscles strengthened not for the mirror, but for the unseen trials ahead. Breath trained not to perform, but to persist. Character formed not for admiration, but for survival.

In the beginning, the work seems slow, even foolish. Others race ahead, collecting attention, gathering applause. But endurance is not a race. It is a quiet laying of stone upon stone, discipline upon discipline, until the inner structure can bear more than the outer world could ever imagine.

Those who build deeper do not hurry. They do not need to. Their work is not for the moment. It is for the seasons yet to come, the storms yet to break, the years yet to demand proof.

They understand that beauty without foundation is fragile. That success without depth is hollow. That life without anchoring cannot hold itself upright when the winds of suffering and change arrive — as they always do.

Foundations are humble things. Hidden things. Forgotten things.

But everything that endures is built upon them.

Enduring structures mirror enduring lives.

What we build is a reflection of who we are.
The strength of a structure is the quiet testament of the one who laid its first stone.

A life that endures is not different from a cathedral that endures. Both are shaped slowly. Both are built with more attention to the unseen than to the visible. Both demand patience that stretches beyond ambition, and care that transcends haste.

An enduring life, like an enduring structure, is not created for display. It is not designed for the approval of the passing crowd. It is constructed for resilience, for storms not yet imagined, for the slow, grinding test of time.

Shaolin understands this parallel. The practitioner does not train simply to perform a form once with beauty, but to live inside the form, to let it weave itself into the way he stands, the way he breathes, the way he moves through the world. He is not building an act. He is building a structure — a life capable of bearing the weight of suffering, the pull of distraction, the pressure of expectation.

Enduring structures are not rigid — they are flexible at their core. They give with the wind but are not undone by it. Enduring lives must be the same. They must hold fast to the essential, but bend with change, move with seasons, survive the unexpected.

There is a humility in both. A recognition that what can be seen is not the test of strength — only what can be sustained is. A loud life, like a fragile structure, may gleam for a while. But a quiet, enduring life holds the real power — to remain when others fall, to stand when others vanish, to continue silently shaping the landscape around it.

In the end, the life you build is the greatest structure you will leave behind.
It will not be remembered for its shine, but for its endurance.

Build it the way the old masters built temples.
Quietly. Patiently. Deep into the ground, deeper still into the soul.
Stone by stone. Breath by breath.

Chapter 9:

Teaching Without Preaching

Influence without imposition.

The deepest lessons are not spoken — they are lived.
They are not pushed upon others — they are offered by presence
alone.

True influence requires no imposition. It moves not by force, but
by example. It demands no audience, no agreement, no applause.
It lives quietly and invites silently.

Shaolin teaches in this way. The Master does not lecture
endlessly. He does not demand obedience through threat or
promise. He moves. He breathes. He stands. He embodies the
teaching before speaking of it, and sometimes, never speaks at all.

The most enduring teachings come not from words but from the
silent consistency of a life lived in alignment with its values. They
are carried in how a person moves through difficulty, in how they
remain steady when the ground shifts, in how they listen when
others speak, in how they hold their silence when others shout.

To teach without preaching is to trust the strength of example
over the weakness of command. It is to understand that the heart
does not open by force — it opens by witnessing something it
recognizes as true.

Those who preach often seek to dominate. They speak loudly because they are unsure. They insist because they doubt. But true influence needs no insistence. It needs only presence — real, unwavering, patient.

Presence does what preaching cannot: it reveals the possibilities without demanding them. It shows the path without pushing others onto it.

A leader who teaches without preaching trusts the student. Trusts that readiness cannot be hurried. Trusts that the lessons worth learning must be chosen freely, not imposed forcefully.

Influence without imposition is not passive. It is powerful in a different way — it respects the autonomy of others, honors their journey, and waits with the quiet certainty that truth, when lived well enough, needs no advertisement.

In the end, the most powerful teaching is not spoken.
It is lived — so completely, so quietly — that it cannot be ignored.

The silent example of the Master.

The Master teaches not through volume, but through presence.
Not through instruction, but through embodiment.
Not through performance, but through being.

In the temple, the Master's lessons are often quiet. He does not interrupt the student's struggle. He does not rush to correct every misstep. He allows the silence to do its work, the repetition to do its carving, the practice to offer its own instruction.

The student watches — not always with understanding at first. They see how the Master moves, how he waits, how he speaks with restraint, how he endures the same disciplines he asks of them. Slowly, without announcement, the lesson reveals itself: you teach not by telling others what to become, but by becoming it yourself.

The Master's life is his curriculum. His conduct is his lecture. His patience is his philosophy. The lessons he cannot articulate with words are the ones that matter most — lessons only seen in the way he responds to failure, the way he respects the invisible labor of practice, the way he greets the world with a steadiness no storm can shake.

Silence is not emptiness. In the Master, it is fullness restrained. It is depth held in reserve.
The students learn not only how to strike or stand; they learn how to endure, how to listen, how to move through the world without the need for noise or approval.

The silent example of the Master transcends the classroom. It reaches into the student's life long after they leave the hall. It becomes the echo in their decisions, the compass in their doubts, the stillness inside their greatest noise.

In the end, they do not remember the speeches.
They remember the man who lived his teaching so completely that even his silence spoke.

The Master teaches not by demanding change, but by embodying it.
Not by preaching truth, but by becoming it.

Living as instruction — wordless leadership.

There is a kind of leadership that requires no speeches, no slogans, no grand displays. It is the leadership of living — the quiet authority that comes from alignment between word and deed, between principle and action.

Wordless leadership is not silent because it has nothing to say; it is silent because it has nothing to prove.

In Shaolin practice, the highest form of instruction is the life lived in plain sight. The Master's stances are not demonstrations; they are expressions of the discipline he practices daily. His patience is not a technique; it is a way of being. His stillness is not a performance; it is his home.

Students watch. They absorb what is not spoken. How the Master bows when no one watches. How he repeats the simplest forms without boredom. How he accepts correction without defensiveness. How he moves through defeat without bitterness and through success without arrogance.

They learn that mastery is not a title you declare — it is a way you live, one quiet choice at a time.

Living as instruction does not impose; it invites. It does not coerce; it inspires. It does not pull others onto a path — it simply walks the path so clearly, so faithfully, that others begin to find their way by its presence alone.

Wordless leadership demands more of the leader. It demands discipline when no one is watching. Integrity when no one is applauding. Consistency when no one is recording. It demands that the life you live be so true that it teaches without speaking.

The loud leader compels compliance. The silent leader cultivates transformation.

Those who lead by living become landmarks. Quiet, steady, immovable. Their presence shapes others more deeply than any command could.

In the end, it is not the leader's words that endure.
It is the life they lived — visible, steady, uncompromising — that remains in the hearts of those they touched.

To teach without preaching is to live the lesson fully enough that no words are required.
Leadership without noise.
Instruction without demand.
Presence without performance.

Chapter 10:
Strength in Service

Power is protection, not domination.

The world mistakes power for dominance. It sees strength as permission to rule, to take, to bend others to the will of the strong.

But true power does not exist to dominate. It exists to protect.

Shaolin teaches this from the first stance. The fists are not clenched to strike first. The forms are not designed for conquest. The strength cultivated is not for the crushing of others, but for the safeguarding of self, of others, of peace.

The warrior is not called to violence; he is called to restraint. His power is not measured by the battles he wins, but by the battles he does not need to fight. By the peace he carries within him — a peace so steady that it shields not only himself but those around him.

Power used for domination corrupts the one who wields it. It makes enemies where there were none. It breaks what it could have protected. It consumes what it could have nurtured.

But power used for protection transforms. It becomes a shelter, not a sword. It becomes a hand extended, not a fist closed. It becomes a quiet assurance to those in its presence: you are safe here, not because I am weak, but because I am strong enough to choose restraint.

In this way, strength becomes service. It is offered, not imposed. It is made available, not flaunted. It is silent until needed, and even when needed, it moves with precision, not with fury.

Shaolin strength is this kind of strength — tempered, steady, compassionate.

The greatest warrior is not the one who defeats the most opponents. It is the one who prevents the fight before it begins. The one whose presence settles the storm before it breaks.

Power is not license to dominate. It is the discipline to protect.

To be strong is not to loom over others.
It is to stand so firmly in your strength that others can stand more safely in theirs.

Leadership begins in service.

Leadership is not ascent; it is descent.
Not rising above others, but lowering yourself into the weight of responsibility for them.

The first instinct of real leadership is not to rule, but to serve.
Not to take more, but to give more.
Not to be seen, but to see.

In Shaolin, the senior student does not simply command the juniors — he tends to them. He corrects not with pride but with care. He leads not by exerting authority, but by exemplifying discipline. He serves the group by ensuring his strength holds space for others to grow.

Leadership without service is hollow. It collapses into vanity. It reduces authority to appearance, power to posture. It consumes instead of cultivates. It demands loyalty without giving trust. It demands labor without offering protection.

But leadership rooted in service is different.
It endures because it is not about the leader. It is about the work, the people, the future being built.

The leader who serves does not seek to be above — he seeks to be beneath, to carry the unseen burdens, to absorb the unseen blows, to make the path smoother for those who follow. He speaks last. He eats last. He takes the blame and gives the credit.

Service is not weakness; it is the highest form of strength. It demands endurance beyond pride. Patience beyond ambition. Humility beyond ego.

To lead in service is to understand that the strength you build is not for your comfort, but for the comfort of others.
The wisdom you gather is not for your elevation, but for the elevation of others.

In the old temples, the statues of great leaders often show them seated, calm, low to the ground — not towering over the world, but rooted deeply within it.
A reminder that real leadership is not in the height you reach, but in the weight you are willing to carry.

Leadership begins where pride ends — in the quiet, demanding place called service.

Compassion is the highest form of strength.

Strength is often misunderstood as hardness — as the ability to resist, to overpower, to endure without bending. But the highest form of strength is not hardness; it is compassion.

Compassion does not soften strength — it deepens it.

In Shaolin, the warrior learns not only how to strike, but when not to strike. Not only how to defeat an opponent, but how to protect one. The ultimate goal is not to destroy, but to preserve. Not to triumph, but to understand. The body is trained to be fierce; the heart is trained to be kind.

Compassion demands more of a person than dominance ever will. It demands that you see beyond yourself. It demands that you hold the pain of others without becoming overwhelmed, that you offer patience when anger would be easier, that you extend understanding when judgment would be quicker.

To be compassionate is to open yourself — not to weakness, but to the kind of courage that refuses to close off in the face of suffering.
It is strength that does not need to prove itself.
Strength that does not need to shout or strike first.
Strength that stands still when provoked, that chooses the harder path of mercy when violence would be faster.

Compassion does not diminish the warrior; it perfects him.
It tempers skill with wisdom.
It transforms power into something greater than force — into care.

The world often admires the cold, the distant, the unfeeling.
But it is not coldness that holds a family together in hard times.
It is not distance that mends a broken community.
It is not indifference that builds the bridges across isolation and fear.
It is compassion — steady, brave, inconvenient compassion — that does these things.

Compassion is not the refusal to fight. It is the fight to remain human in a world that forgets what humanity requires.
It is the choice, again and again, to meet the world not with fear, but with an open hand.
Not because it is easy, but because it is strong.

In the end, the greatest mark of strength is not how much you can carry, but how much you can care.

Chapter 11:

Stillness in Leadership

Leadership without losing your center.

Leadership, when misunderstood, becomes a slow erosion of self. The weight of responsibility, the noise of expectation, the unrelenting demands of others — these forces press inward, threatening to pull the leader away from the center they once fought to build.

Many lose themselves here. They become fractured by the needs they cannot meet, pulled in too many directions to remember their own. Leadership, instead of magnifying their clarity, becomes the very thing that blurs it.

Shaolin teaches differently. In the temple, strength begins in stillness. Movement follows only when stillness is intact. The leader who forgets this — who moves first, who responds first, who acts without anchoring — is a leader who will be lost.

Stillness is not absence of motion; it is presence within motion. It is the internal anchor that holds when everything outside is shifting.
It is the quiet within the noise, the calm within the current.

To lead without losing your center is to remain tethered to what cannot be negotiated — to principle, to clarity, to truth. It is to refuse to lead by mere reaction. It is to refuse to chase every crisis, to panic at every turn, to sacrifice integrity for applause or expedience.

The true leader does not hurry their mind, even if the world hurries its demands.
They do not scatter their heart, even if the world tries to pull it apart.

They move from stillness — so that each action is clean, each decision is clear, each word is measured. They listen without rushing to fix. They wait without surrendering to pressure. They act without losing themselves in the action.

A leader without stillness becomes hollow — a figurehead for the chaos around them.
A leader with stillness becomes a ground — a steady point others can gather around, draw from, trust in.

The storms will come. The noise will rise. The demands will multiply.

The only way to lead through them is not to move faster — but to root deeper.
Not to lose yourself — but to remain at the center you built long before others called you to lead.

Bearing responsibility without bearing ego.

Responsibility and ego are often confused.
One is the acceptance of weight.
The other is the craving for it.

To bear responsibility is to carry what must be carried — the decisions, the consequences, the burdens no one else can or will hold. It is to accept that leadership is not about power, but about weight — the invisible load of care, of foresight, of sacrifice.

But ego transforms responsibility into something else.
It turns service into spectacle.
It makes leadership about the leader — about being seen, being praised, being central to everything that moves.

Shaolin teaches the separation early. The novice carries water not to be noticed, but because water must be carried. The Master accepts the discipline not for admiration, but because discipline is the path. Nothing is done for appearance. Everything is done for necessity, for principle.

Leadership without ego is quiet. It moves without the need for attention. It carries without the need for recognition. It acts, not to be known, but because action is needed.

The leader who sheds ego carries more, but feels lighter.
Because they do not drag the heavy need to be admired alongside the true burdens they hold.

Ego corrupts responsibility. It makes it personal, transactional.
It demands repayment — loyalty, applause, gratitude.
But real responsibility asks for nothing back. It is an offering, not an exchange.

To bear responsibility without bearing ego is to be free.
Free to serve without resentment.
Free to act without posturing.
Free to lead without distorting the very path you are called to walk.

The ego says, "I am the reason."
The responsible leader says, "I am the servant."

And because of this, they can remain still even under the heaviest weight — steady, humble, invisible when necessary, present always.

Real leadership is not the aggrandizement of self — it is the disappearance of it.

The leader becomes not the centerpiece of the work, but the ground it quietly grows from.

Remaining yourself as the weight grows.

The greater the weight, the greater the temptation to become something else.
To bend under the load.
To shape yourself to the expectations of others.
To compromise the quiet truths you once held when the path was lighter and the journey less demanding.

Leadership tests not only your skill but your identity.
It asks: can you remain who you are when the burden grows

heavier?

When more eyes are watching, more hands are pulling, more noise is pressing in from all sides?

Many start strong and clear.
But as the weight grows, so does the temptation to trade authenticity for approval, conviction for comfort, presence for performance.
Slowly, almost imperceptibly, the leader becomes unrecognizable — to others, and eventually, to themselves.

Shaolin discipline is built against this erosion.
The forms are repeated not because they change, but because they don't.
The breath is returned to, again and again, because its rhythm remains true even when the body tires, even when the mind wavers.

The principle is simple: when the world grows heavy, return to what is simple.
When the noise grows loud, return to what is quiet.
When the demands grow large, return to what is small — breath, step, stillness.

Remaining yourself is not stubbornness.
It is fidelity — to the deeper current of who you are beneath the titles, beneath the expectations, beneath the weight.

It means refusing to perform a version of yourself that is more acceptable but less true.
It means remembering the discipline, the patience, the clarity that existed before the world noticed, before the responsibilities grew, before the burden felt endless.

The greatest leaders are not those who bend themselves to match the shape of the weight.
They are those who let the weight sharpen them, deepen them, but never change their root.

Stillness is the anchor.
Without it, you drift — no matter how capable, no matter how admired.

With it, you remain — steady as the burden grows, yourself even as the seasons change.

A leader does not lead by becoming what the world demands.
A leader leads by remaining who the path demands — true, quiet, unwavering.

Chapter 12:

Presence Over Performance

Resist the lure of appearances.

The world trains us to perform.
It teaches us early that appearances are currency — that being
seen is being valued, that being praised is being right, that being
noticed is being worthy.

But performance is a hollow currency.
It buys attention, but not depth.
It earns applause, but not peace.

Shaolin training cuts against this grain.
The forms are not rehearsed for spectacle; they are repeated for
understanding.
The movements are not choreographed for admiration; they are
lived, slowly, quietly, until they become part of the one who
practices them.

Performance seeks to be seen.
Presence seeks to be true.

The performer moves outward — adjusting, posing, reshaping
themselves to the demands of the crowd.
The one anchored in presence moves inward — acting from
alignment, not expectation; from conviction, not applause.

To resist the lure of appearances is not to reject excellence — it is to reject pretending.
It is to stand in the quiet discipline of authenticity when pretense would be easier, more rewarded, more celebrated.

It demands that you remember who you are without the mirror of public opinion.
It demands that you build a life that is steady even when unseen, even when misunderstood, even when overlooked.

Appearances will always call to you.
The easy lure of being admired, the soft seduction of being approved.
But their price is high — they cost you your peace, your clarity, your self-respect.

Presence asks a harder thing:
To be fully yourself whether or not anyone notices.
To do the work even when no one is watching.
To walk the path even when no one applauds.

Presence is quiet.
But it is the only thing that endures when the lights fade and the crowds move on.

Resist the lure of appearances.
Return to the discipline of presence.

Be seen without seeking to be seen.

There is a difference between being seen and seeking to be seen.
One is a byproduct of living fully; the other is a substitute for it.

To be seen without seeking it is to live in such a way that your
presence cannot help but register — not because you chased
attention, but because you moved with clarity, with weight, with
truth.

Shaolin practice teaches this subtly.
The Master does not parade his strength; it reveals itself without
effort.
The precision of his movements, the depth of his stillness, the
steadiness of his breath — these things are not performed, they
are lived.
And because they are lived so deeply, they are seen without ever
needing to be shown.

The world tempts you to invert this — to seek attention first and
meaning later.
To live in pursuit of eyes rather than in pursuit of mastery.
To craft an image rather than build a life.

But what is chased rarely satisfies.
The attention you seek will not feed you.
The applause you engineer will not anchor you.

Presence does not chase attention.
It carries itself.
It fills a room not with noise, but with gravity.

To be seen without seeking it is to focus entirely on the work, the discipline, the becoming — and to let whatever notice comes be incidental, not intentional.

It is to stand still inside your life while others rush to broadcast theirs.
It is to deepen the root rather than decorate the branch.

Those who are truly present are seen not for their performance, but for their substance.
And when they are seen, it is not the person who shouts the loudest that we remember — it is the one who moved with quiet authority, who carried something heavier than approval, something truer than admiration.

You do not need to chase being seen.
Live fully, deeply, honestly — and presence will do the rest.

Anchor presence deeper than performance.

Performance is thin. It rises quickly and fades just as fast.
It is a wave that depends on the reaction of others to stay alive.
When the audience leaves, the performance dissolves.

Presence is different. It does not rely on being seen. It does not swell when praised or shrink when ignored.
It is anchored deeper — below applause, below recognition, below the need to be validated at all.

Shaolin practice is a study in this difference.
The early movements feel like performance — imitating the master, mimicking the form.
But as the training deepens, the student discovers that the true power lies not in the external appearance of the movement, but in its internal rooting.
A stance that is deep not in display, but in structure.
A breath that is steady not for others to notice, but because it must be steady to endure.

Presence must be anchored the same way.
It must be rooted deeper than image.
Deeper than reaction.
Deeper than outcome.

If it is not, it will always be at risk — vulnerable to every slight, every criticism, every shift in public opinion.

To anchor presence is to tie it to something immovable — to principle, to discipline, to truth.
It is to know who you are without needing others to confirm it.
It is to move, to speak, to build, not for recognition but because the action itself is aligned with who you are.

Presence rooted in this way has a different weight.
It lingers.
It steadies others without needing to announce itself.
It fills the space it occupies without noise, without demand.

Performance may impress the surface;
Presence transforms the depth.

The greatest leaders, the truest warriors, the most enduring creators — they anchor their presence in something the world cannot touch.

And because of this, they do not fade when the applause ends.
They remain.

Anchor presence deeper than performance.
Root it where it cannot be shaken.

Chapter 13:

Letting the Work Go

Clinging destroys what was built.

It is a strange truth: what you grip too tightly, you risk breaking.
What you refuse to release, you begin to crush.
What you cannot let go of — even your finest work — begins,
silently, to die in your hands.

Shaolin practice teaches the discipline of release.
A strike that holds tension too long loses its power.
A stance gripped too rigidly collapses under its own weight.
Even mastery, if clung to with desperation, becomes a trap —
binding the master to what should have been a gift.

The work you build must be held lightly if it is to live.
You shape it, yes — with care, with precision, with patience.
But you do not own it. You do not possess it. You do not lock it in
the cage of your own ego.

Clinging is born from fear — the fear of loss, of irrelevance, of
being forgotten.
But what is clung to does not stay preserved; it begins to decay.

The tree that holds its leaves too long does not survive the winter.
The river that refuses to flow becomes stagnant.
The master who cannot release his craft becomes a relic, not a
living teacher.

To let go is not to discard. It is to trust.
To trust that what you have built can live without your constant grasp.
To trust that its life extends beyond your control, that its purpose exceeds your presence.

Letting go does not dishonor the work — it honors it more deeply.
It gives it the freedom to grow, to adapt, to endure without you.

Clinging seeks to immortalize the self.
Letting go seeks to serve something larger.

If you love what you have made, you must one day loosen your hands and let it move into the world without you.

And in doing so, you will find the paradox:
What you let go of fully is what lasts the longest.
What you release is what returns.

Clinging destroys what was built.
Letting go allows it to live.

Release is part of mastery.

Mastery is not only about creation.
It is also about release.

To build something skillfully is one achievement.
To let it go gracefully is a higher one.

The world celebrates the making — the forging of a craft, the rise of a leader, the creation of a work.
But it often neglects the quieter, harder truth: that mastery is not complete until the maker learns to step back.
Until the builder trusts what he has built enough to stop clutching it.
Until the master trusts his students enough to leave them.

In Shaolin, release is woven into the practice.
The student, once taught, must be trusted to move without constant guidance.
The form, once mastered, must be allowed to evolve beyond the teacher's hand.
The knowledge, once given, must be released into the world without being controlled.

Mastery does not mean holding forever.
It means knowing when the holding must end.

Release is not abdication — it is an act of faith.
It says: what I have shaped is now strong enough to stand on its own.
What I have taught is now deep enough to endure without me.

To release is to recognize that the work is not you.
It is not your identity.
It is not your possession.

It is something that passed through you — shaped by your hands, yes — but never truly yours to imprison.

Release is the final movement of mastery because it completes the cycle.
Creation, refinement, offering — and finally, release.

Only those who have mastered their own need to cling are truly free to create without fear and to let go without loss.

Release is not the opposite of mastery.
It is the proof of it.

Letting go so the work may live.

The work you create is not meant to be an extension of your control.
It is meant to have a life beyond you.

If you grip it too tightly, it will never breathe on its own.
If you insist on owning every outcome, dictating every path, defending every change, you will smother the very thing you hoped would endure.

Letting go is not abandonment — it is permission.
Permission for the work to evolve.
Permission for those who come after you to make it their own.
Permission for the seed you planted to grow into something you could not predict — something larger, wilder, freer than your original design.

Shaolin teaches this without saying it aloud.
The teacher passes on the form, but does not fossilize it.
The Master releases the student not when they are perfect, but when they are ready to discover the rest themselves.
The tradition survives not because it is clutched tightly, but

because it is allowed to flow from generation to generation, each adding breath to what came before.

If the work is worthy, it will not need you to control it.
It will find new life through other hands, other voices, other hearts.

Letting go is hard because it feels like loss.
But it is not loss — it is a greater kind of creation.
It is the creation of something that can survive without your constant tending, something that can carry its own weight, something that will walk into places you cannot go and outlive days you will not see.

This is the mark of real legacy:
Not that you controlled the work, but that you freed it.

Not that it stayed as you left it, but that it grew because you trusted it to.

Letting go is not giving up.
It is giving forward.

If you wish the work to live, you must learn to let it go.

Chapter 14:

Moving Through, Not Against

Seasons change — mastery flows with them.

Nothing in nature resists the season it inhabits.
The river does not argue with winter's freeze or summer's drought.
The tree does not cling to its leaves when autumn calls them down.
The mountain does not defy the slow carving of wind and rain.

Everything that endures does so not by fighting the seasons, but by flowing with them.

Shaolin practice is a study in this acceptance.
Forms change as the body changes.
Breath changes as the moment demands.
The mind is taught not to resist impermanence, but to move with it — to adapt, to adjust, to endure not by rigidity, but by flexibility.

Mastery does not cling to old rhythms when new ones are called for.
It does not mourn the fading of a season or deny the arrival of another.
It flows — not passively, not weakly, but willingly, wisely.

The greatest strength is not stubbornness.
It is adaptability.

The master who cannot adapt becomes a monument — admired, perhaps, but unmoving, and soon irrelevant.
The master who flows with the seasons remains alive — present, responsive, enduring.

Life demands this same wisdom.
The seasons will change whether or not you are ready.
Circumstances will shift.
Roles will end.
Stages will close.
The ones who endure are not the ones who resist these changes with clenched fists, but the ones who open their hands, adjust their stance, and move forward with the new current.

To master life is not to master the seasons.
It is to master the art of moving through them.

To move through is to remain yourself while letting go of what no longer fits.
It is to keep your root while bending with the wind.

Those who learn to move through the seasons do not fear change — they welcome it.
They do not mourn endings — they honor them.
They do not resist the inevitable — they ride it.

In this way, they remain — not frozen, not broken — but alive, growing, free.

Mastery flows.
Always.

Resistance exhausts — adaptation endures.

To resist what must happen is to exhaust yourself.
It is to waste your strength in battles you cannot win, to spend your energy holding walls that will fall no matter how tightly you grip them.

Resistance consumes.
Adaptation conserves.

Shaolin teaches this early, not in words but in movement.
A rigid body tires quickly; a flexible one endures.
A mind that stiffens against every challenge cracks under the weight of life; a mind that bends, that flows, survives what others cannot.

To resist every change is to live in a constant state of friction.
You pull against the river instead of learning to ride it.
You cling to what must be released.
You mourn what is already gone.
You fight time itself — and time, undefeated, moves forward without you.

Adaptation is different.
It is not surrender.
It is not weakness.
It is the choice to remain in motion, even when the path bends sharply and the ground shifts beneath you.

Adaptation asks: what is the heart of who I am that cannot be compromised?
And what are the outer forms that must change if I am to endure?

It asks you to loosen your grip on what no longer serves.
It invites you to meet the world as it is, not as you wish it were.

Those who resist grow weary long before the race is done.
Those who adapt move quietly past them — not faster, but longer,
not harder, but wiser.

Adaptation protects what matters most by refusing to waste
energy on what cannot be saved.
It shields the root by letting the branches bend.
It protects the fire by adjusting the sails when the wind changes.

Life is not impressed by your resistance.
It is not moved by your refusal to change.
It will keep shifting with or without you.

The wise do not exhaust themselves fighting what must happen.
They conserve their strength by learning to move with it.

Resistance exhausts.
Adaptation endures.

Endurance through quiet change.

Change does not always announce itself with thunder.
Sometimes it arrives like mist — soft, slow, inevitable.

Those who endure are not always the ones who fight loudly or
declare their defiance against the coming storm.
Often, they are the ones who change quietly — without spectacle,
without struggle, without losing the thread of who they are.

In Shaolin practice, change is not resisted; it is absorbed.
The body shifts stance without hesitation.
The breath adjusts to the rhythm of the moment.
The mind releases the old form to enter the new.

No declarations, no drama — just the quiet pivot, the silent
adaptation, the small yielding that protects the larger strength.

This kind of quiet change is not weakness.
It is a deeper form of endurance — one that bends without
breaking, one that moves without losing itself, one that continues
even when everything familiar falls away.

To endure through quiet change is to accept that not every
adaptation must be announced.
Not every evolution must be explained.
Some changes are private, internal, known only to the one who
carries them — and it is precisely this inward shift that preserves
the heart against the erosion of time.

The loud resist until they collapse.
The wise adjust without needing applause for their resilience.

They change not because they have given up, but because they
have chosen to survive.
They yield not because they are weak, but because they
understand that endurance demands movement — small, patient,
continuous.

They let go of what must be let go.
They carry forward what must be carried.
They remain not because they have fought harder, but because
they have adapted quieter.

Quiet change is the secret of those who last.
It is the hidden strength of those who seem, to the untrained eye,
unshaken by what would undo others.

They are not unchanged.
They are not untouched.

They are simply unbroken — because they moved through, not
against.

Chapter 15:

Becoming Invisible Again

The Shifu's final lesson: leave no trace.

In the beginning, the journey is visible.
You strive. You build. You push forward with weight and motion,
leaving marks behind — achievements, creations, echoes of
effort.

But mastery carries a different ending.
It asks not for more marks, but for their quiet erasure.
It asks not to be remembered for the weight you imposed, but for
the space you protected.

Shaolin teaches this final lesson softly.
The true Master fades.
He does not cling to titles.
He does not anchor himself in reputation.
He steps back into the background he once emerged from,
trusting that what he built no longer needs his hand to stand.

Leave no trace — not because you did not move, but because you
moved so carefully, so completely, that the world continues
undisturbed when you are gone.

In the mountains, the river carves the stone for centuries and then
disappears.
The bamboo bends and yields without leaving scars.

The seasons change, the winds shift, and the forest remains —
altered, but whole.

The greatest impact is often the one that cannot be seen directly.
It is carried in the lives touched, the ideas planted, the strength
given quietly and without fanfare.

To leave no trace is not to erase your work — it is to refuse to
chain yourself to it.
It is to trust that what you have given was never meant to bear
your name forever.

The ego fears this disappearance.
It clings to legacy, to memory, to monuments.
But the Master knows: to truly endure is to vanish into the life of
the work itself.

The Shifu's final lesson is disappearance.
The stepping back.   -
The return to stillness.
The silence after the song that allows the song to echo longer than
the singer's voice.

Leave no trace — and in doing so, leave everything that matters.

Mastery retreats into simplicity.

The longer you walk the path, the less you need.

At the beginning, there is complexity — techniques to learn,
knowledge to gather, disciplines to stack high upon one another.

The mind is full, the hands are busy, the days are crowded with striving.

But true mastery does not end in complexity.
It ends in simplicity.

Shaolin shows this in every movement.
The Master's form, once intricate and sprawling, becomes spare.
The steps are fewer, but deeper.
The motions are simpler, but fuller.
There is less — but what remains carries all the weight that matters.

Mastery is a process of reduction.
It is not adding more, but shedding what is no longer essential.
It is the slow, quiet return to the few things that matter most —
discipline, breath, presence, humility.

Simplicity is not emptiness.
It is clarity.
It is power unadorned.
It is knowing exactly what needs to be done and doing only that.

Those who are early in the journey confuse movement with meaning.
They accumulate.
They decorate.
They announce.

But the Master, nearing the end of the journey, sheds all that.
He does not accumulate; he refines.
He does not decorate; he distills.
He does not announce; he moves in silence.

Mastery retreats into simplicity because it understands that true strength needs no ornament, that real wisdom needs no noise, that lasting presence needs no performance.

It knows that the highest form of movement is stillness.
The highest form of speech is silence.
The highest form of achievement is not needing to be seen.

To master anything is to arrive at the place where almost nothing is needed, and everything that remains is real.

Mastery retreats — not in defeat, but in fulfillment.

It leaves behind the layers, the masks, the clutter.

It returns to what was there at the beginning — breath, body, mind — only now understood, now lived fully, now silent.

Simplicity is not the absence of mastery.
It is its final and most enduring form.

The work endures — the master disappears.

At the end, the Master does not stand atop his creation, arms raised in triumph.
He steps away.
Quietly, without ceremony, without demand.

He knows that the true measure of the work is not how brightly he shines beside it, but how long it can stand without him.

The ego longs to remain attached — to leave a name etched into stone, to ensure the world remembers who built what.
But the Master knows better.
He knows that real work must be released from its maker to fully live.
That the greatest testament to his labor is not eternal applause, but silent endurance.

Shaolin teaches this without ever speaking it aloud.
The Master trains the students, knowing they will one day outgrow his instruction.
He builds the temple, knowing it must stand without his constant tending.
He carries the tradition, knowing that to preserve it, he must let it evolve without needing to stamp his identity upon it.

The work is not an extension of the self.
It is a gift — and gifts must be given freely.

When the Master disappears, the work remains.
It breathes through the hands of those he taught.
It moves through the lives he touched.
It ripples outward, unbound by the smallness of personal legacy.

The master's face fades.
The voice grows quiet.
The name is spoken less often.

But the work — the real work — deepens, strengthens, persists.

The Master does not fear this fading.
He welcomes it.
Because he understands: to remain visible forever would be to limit what he built to his own lifetime, his own shadow.

By disappearing, he allows the work to grow beyond him —
untethered, unconfined, alive.

The river forgets the rain that fed it.
The tree forgets the hand that planted it.
And this is as it should be.

The master disappears.
The work endures.

This is how it must be — and how it was always meant to be.

What Now

Stillness is not a crown worn.
It is a river carried — silent, unseen, enduring.

The disciplines you have built — patience, breath, restraint,
presence — are not an escape from life's weight.
They are the quiet preparation for bearing it fully.

A mountain does not prove its height in clear weather.
It proves its endurance under storm, under wind, under time.

In the same way, the stillness cultivated in solitude is not proven
by remaining apart from the world.
It is proven by returning to it — intact, unchanged at the root,
even as the world tries to move you.

The breath you have guarded must now remain steady under
pressure.
The silence you have practiced must now withstand the noise.
The leadership you have learned must now carry weight without
seeking recognition.
The endurance you have strengthened must now be tested by loss,
by betrayal, by seasons of loneliness and unseen labor.

The world will not recognize the gate you carry.
It will not honor your patience.
It will not respect your quiet strength.

It will press against it.
It will try to move it.
It will demand noise where you have learned silence.

It will demand speed where you have trained patience.
It will demand surrender where you have built presence.

You must move through this — not untouched, but unbroken.
Not protected, but preserved.

The gate was never meant to be an escape.
It was meant to be a threshold carried with you — visible only in the way you remain yourself while others dissolve.

The mountain bends to no storm.
The river carves stone not by force, but by endurance.

You are not finished.
You are not safe.
You are ready.

What was built quietly must now be tested fully.
What was learned in stillness must now move through the fire — not to destroy it, but to deepen it.

The breath continues.
The path continues.
There is no arrival — only the next motion, and the stillness carried within it.

Chapter 16:
Conflict Without Collapse

The Nature of Conflict

Conflict is not an interruption of life.
It is life.

It arrives not because something has gone wrong, but because the nature of the world is movement — and wherever there is movement, there is friction.
Where there are boundaries, there will be pressure.
Where there is selfhood, there will be challenge.

Stillness is not the absence of conflict.
It is the refusal to be moved by it.

The one who seeks only peace is not seeking mastery.
He is seeking retreat.
The one who demands a life without struggle is not walking the path.
He is hiding from it.

Shaolin discipline does not prepare the student for a world without storms.
It teaches him to endure them — not with rigid resistance that snaps under force, but with anchored patience that bends and holds and survives.

Conflict, like weather, is neither enemy nor ally.
It is condition.
It is the breath of the world in opposition to your own breath —
not to destroy it, but to shape it, to test it, to deepen it.

A Shifu does not fear conflict.
Nor does he worship it.
He accepts it — not as something to be chased, not as something
to be avoided, but as something to be understood.

To live without collapse, one must understand the nature of
conflict:

It is not personal.
It is not final.
It is not even about you.

It is the friction of living things against each other, of ambitions
colliding, of wills pressing, of seasons shifting.

The master does not imagine himself above conflict.
He simply learns not to add unnecessary heat to it.
He does not resist the pressure — he adjusts to it.
He does not dissolve into the noise — he stands within it, quiet,
deliberate, unshaken.

In this way, conflict becomes not a force of destruction, but a
forge.

The heat rises.
The breath shortens.
The voices sharpen.
The hands tremble.

And the Shifu stands still — not because he is immune, but
because he is anchored.

Stillness does not make conflict disappear.
It makes collapse unnecessary.

The world moves against him, but he does not move against himself.

This is the first lesson of endurance under fire:
Conflict is not your enemy.
Collapse is.

Holding Stillness Under Attack

Attack reveals the substance of stillness.
It strips away the appearance of calm and leaves only what is real.

In solitude, stillness can seem effortless — a matter of quiet, of setting, of breath.
But under attack, stillness is exposed.
It is no longer protected by silence or distance.
It is pressed, tested, pushed to the edge of collapse.

The world does not test stillness with gentle hands.
It tests it with insult, with injustice, with misunderstanding, with betrayal.
It tests it with chaos — words sharpened into weapons,
movements meant to provoke, energies designed to unmake what was patiently built.

In these moments, the instinct is to react — to defend the self with noise, to answer force with force, to meet pressure with panic.

But reaction is collapse.
It is the breaking of the internal foundation under external weight.

Stillness under attack does not resist blindly.
It does not meet anger with anger, noise with noise, aggression with fear.

It absorbs.

It allows the attack to pass through —
not because it is weak, but because it is not centered on the self.

Stillness does not answer every insult.
It does not parry every blow.
It does not race to be understood, or validated, or proven right.

It remains — unhurried, unshaken, undiminished.

The Shifu standing under attack is not numb.
He feels the sting of words, the injustice of false accusation, the strain of being misunderstood.
But he does not act from these feelings.

He waits.

Not for permission, not for approval —
for the storm to spend itself.

Attack requires reaction to succeed.
It feeds on the energy it provokes.

Stillness denies it that energy.

It is not passivity.
It is not surrender.

It is deliberate non-collapse — a choice to remain intact even as the world around fractures and howls.

To hold stillness under attack is to accept the heat without adding to it.
It is to feel the full weight of provocation and yet move from principle, not from pressure.

The mind calms the breath.
The breath anchors the body.
The body stills the motion.
The motion protects the mind.

In this way, stillness becomes a fortress invisible to the attacker — a quiet refusal to be broken.

The attack passes.
The storm fades.
And the Shifu remains — not because he fought harder, but because he did not lose himself.

Stillness is not the absence of conflict.
It is the absence of collapse.

Quiet Power

Power does not need to announce itself.
True power, like deep water, moves with weight but without noise.

The world is filled with loud strength — the kind that shouts, that demands recognition, that seeks to dominate through display.

It is an exhausting strength, always searching for proof, always hungry for affirmation.

But the Shifu carries a different kind of power —
one that does not require attention to exist.
One that endures, invisible to those who look only for spectacle.

Quiet power is not weakness hidden.
It is strength refined.

It is the knowledge that real influence comes not from force, but from presence — the silent gravity of someone who cannot be moved, no matter how the winds shift.

The warrior without discipline believes that victory is in the blow struck, the enemy defeated.
The master knows that the highest victory is not needing to strike at all.
That presence alone can end a conflict before it begins.

This power is not easily won.
It is built — layer upon layer, breath upon breath, failure upon failure — until the foundation is deep enough to hold the full weight of conflict without buckling.

Quiet power is patience under pressure.
It is endurance without bitterness.
It is certainty without arrogance.
It is strength that does not rise and fall with circumstance.

In the moment of conflict, it is not the loudest voice that leads.
It is the voice that remains steady when others break.

It is not the one who moves first who wins.
It is the one who moves last —

not from exhaustion, not from fear, but from clarity, from deliberate restraint.

Quiet power does not collapse under attack because it has no illusions to defend.
It does not depend on recognition, approval, or victory to exist.

It simply is —
anchored, steady, enduring.

The Shifu who holds quiet power does not dominate the field.
He does not need to.

His presence changes the shape of conflict.
His stillness disrupts the momentum of attack.
His calm becomes a mirror in which the noise reveals itself as emptiness.

And when the storm passes, when the voices fall silent, when the dust settles —
it is the quiet one who remains,
intact, unbroken,
not because he fought harder, but because he refused to be moved.

This is quiet power:
Strength that cannot be seen — only felt.
Stillness that cannot be shaken — only endured.

The true master does not collapse under conflict.
He carries the breath he began with —
steady, unhurried, unbroken —
into every storm.

Chapter 17:

Loss Without Breaking

Loss as a True Test

It is easy to remain whole when nothing has been taken from you.
It is easy to speak of endurance in seasons of abundance, to
practice patience when the stakes are low, to cultivate calm when
the ground is steady.

But loss exposes what ease can conceal.
It strips away the comforts that shield the untested mind.
It demands not theory, but reality — not aspiration, but substance.

Loss is not failure.
It is a mirror.

It reflects back what discipline has truly built, or failed to build.
It shows whether stillness is real, or merely a posture maintained
in favorable weather.
It reveals whether presence can survive when the anchors of
comfort and success are cut away.

A Shifu does not seek loss.
But he does not fear it.
He understands that loss is not an enemy to be avoided, but a
terrain to be crossed — slowly, deliberately, without collapse.

The disciple who believes that mastery will protect him from loss has misunderstood the nature of the path.
Mastery does not prevent loss.
It prevents loss from breaking the master.

Stillness is not insulation from pain.
It is the refusal to let pain define the self.

Loss may take much — reputation, position, fortune, even the quiet structures of daily life — but it cannot take the discipline patiently built within.
Unless you allow it.

What cannot be lost is what has been internalized — not worn like armor, but grown like bone.

Loss is not proof of inadequacy.
It is proof of life.
To love, to build, to strive — all these make loss inevitable.
The goal is not to live carefully enough to avoid it, but to live deeply enough to survive it without bitterness.

The root must run deeper than the weather can reach.
The breath must continue even as the winds rise.

In loss, many collapse because they built only on the visible: titles, possessions, reputations, outcomes.
When these are stripped away, nothing remains to hold them upright.

The Shifu builds on the invisible —
discipline without applause, endurance without reward, presence without validation.

When loss comes — as it always does —
he does not break because he was never resting on what loss can touch.

The foundation remains.
The breath continues.
The path endures.

Loss is not the end of the discipline.
It is its true beginning.

Enduring the Weight of Grief

Grief is not a failure of discipline.
It is its true weight.

There are losses that cannot be reasoned with, that cannot be softened by wisdom or endurance.
There are blows that strike not the surface of life, but its foundation — losses that tear at the roots, not the branches.

To endure grief is not to escape its pain.
It is to refuse to collapse under it.

Stillness does not deny sorrow.
It carries it — slowly, carefully, as one carries a vessel filled to the brim, knowing that a sudden movement would spill it all.

The Shifu understands that grief cannot be conquered.
It must be endured.

Endurance is not numbness.
It is not the absence of feeling.
It is the ability to remain present to the weight of sorrow without letting it destroy the self that carries it.

Grief demands slowness.
It demands breath drawn deeply, movements made carefully, days lived with deliberate patience.

The undisciplined mind seeks escape — in noise, in anger, in endless motion.
But these are only temporary shelters, destined to crumble.

The disciplined mind does not run.
It does not rage against what cannot be undone.
It sits with grief — not as a passive victim, but as a witness.
It allows sorrow its place, but not its dominion.

In Shaolin practice, the body is trained to hold strain without collapse, to remain in stance long after the muscles begin to tremble.
Grief is the same test — but for the soul.

It shakes the internal foundation.
It demands endurance not in performance, but in patience.
Not in movement, but in stillness.

Grief is not something to be outpaced.
It is something to be carried.

The weight does not lessen because you resist it.
It lessens because you learn to bear it without breaking.

The one who endures grief without collapsing does not emerge unmarked.

Grief leaves its shape on the heart, just as water leaves its mark on stone.

But the mark is not damage.
It is depth.

The Shifu who has carried grief without collapse carries a different stillness.
A stillness that is not untouched by sorrow, but tempered by it.
A stillness that has learned to breathe in thinner air.

Grief does not end.
It only changes its weight.

Stillness does not erase the loss.
It teaches you how to live with it — carefully, patiently, quietly — without being undone.

Continuation Without Resolution

There are losses that do not resolve.
There are wounds that do not close.

The mind, trained by the world, seeks closure — a neat ending, a final explanation, a moment when the weight lifts and the path clears.
But discipline teaches something harsher, and truer:
some burdens are not lifted.
They are carried.

Stillness does not promise resolution.
It promises endurance.

The world demands that pain be overcome, that grief be conquered, that sorrow be outgrown.
But the master knows that the deepest wounds are not victories waiting to be claimed.
They are companions — unwelcome, heavy, permanent.

To continue without resolution is not weakness.
It is the highest form of strength.

It is the quiet decision to move forward not because the path is clear, but because the path exists — and must be walked.

The river does not wait for the storm to pass before it flows.
It moves through rain, through flood, through drought.
It continues not because conditions are favorable, but because its nature is to move.

The Shifu does not continue because the sorrow has lessened, or the loss has explained itself.
He continues because he must.
Because the breath must be carried forward.
Because presence demands not understanding, but endurance.

This is not stoicism hardened into numbness.
It is not the refusal to feel.
It is the willingness to feel fully — and to move anyway.

The undisciplined spirit collapses in the absence of resolution.
It demands certainty, justice, fairness.
It will not step until the ground feels solid.

But the disciplined spirit accepts uncertainty.
It moves even when the ground shifts.

It breathes even when the air is thin.
It endures even when the destination is lost to view.

Continuation without resolution is the final proof of stillness.
It is the breath drawn not because it brings comfort, but because it
is necessary.
It is the step taken not because the way is easy, but because it is
right.

The world will not reward this kind of endurance.
It will not see it.
But the master does not move for reward.
He moves because the breath continues.
Because the work remains.
Because the discipline endures even when all else falls away.

Resolution is a comfort.
Endurance is a way.

The Shifu does not wait for peace to move.
He carries the sorrow, the uncertainty, the loss — carefully,
patiently — and moves anyway.

Stillness is not resolution.
It is continuation — without end.

Chapter 18:

Power Without Corruption

Authority as Burden

Power is a test few recognize and fewer survive.
It does not test strength or skill or even endurance.
It tests the root — the quiet place inside the self where discipline
must be deeper than ambition, and restraint stronger than desire.

Authority appears, at first, as reward.
It comes dressed in the garments of recognition, influence, voice.
But for the one who understands the path, it is not reward.
It is burden.

The untrained spirit sees power as elevation.
The disciplined spirit sees it as weight.

Shaolin practice teaches the body to carry strain — stance after
stance, form after form — until the legs tremble, the breath
shortens, and the will must decide whether to endure or collapse.
Authority is the same training — but for the soul.

Leadership, influence, power — these are not privileges.
They are tests of the ability to remain disciplined when no one
can enforce it but yourself.

Without discipline, power corrupts not by making a man worse,
but by revealing what was shallow all along.

It amplifies what is already there: insecurity, vanity, hunger for recognition.
It magnifies the cracks the world was too quiet to expose before.

A Shifu does not seek authority.
He accepts it when necessary — not as a prize, but as a responsibility.

To lead without being led by the hunger for power requires more than skill.
It requires the internal clarity to see authority not as elevation above others, but as deeper service to them.

Authority demands that you act without needing to be seen.
It demands that you serve without expectation of gratitude.
It demands that you endure misunderstanding, resistance, even betrayal — without abandoning the work or the discipline that sustains it.

The burden of authority is not that you are followed.
It is that you must walk without being carried by praise or approval.

True power is not in having followers.
It is in refusing to need them.

The Shifu does not collapse under authority because he never allowed authority to become his identity.
He leads because there is work to be done.
He endures the burden of power because the path demands it — not because it affirms him.

Authority is not a crown.
It is a weight.
And it must be carried carefully — like a vessel filled to the edge — lest it spill and undo the work it was meant to protect.

The burden will not grow lighter.
But you will grow stronger — not in stature, but in stillness.

The master is not the one who seizes power.
He is the one who bears it without collapse.

The Corrosion of Ego

Ego is not loud when it first enters.
It is quiet, subtle, reasonable.

It whispers that recognition is deserved, that influence is earned,
that leadership should come with reward.
It convinces the heart that acceptance is loyalty, that gratitude is a
measure of worth, that applause is proof of value.

Ego does not corrupt all at once.
It corrodes — slowly, invisibly — wearing away discipline grain
by grain.

The Shifu is not immune.
He feels the pull, the temptation to believe the authority he holds
is confirmation of superiority rather than a call to deeper humility.
He hears the echo of praise and must decide whether to listen or
to let it pass through him, as wind through trees.

Shaolin teaches that the hardest enemy is the one who looks like a
friend.
Ego is this enemy.

It arrives dressed as affirmation, but it demands your surrender.
It promises security, but it trades it for dependence.
It offers applause, but it chains the spirit to needing more.

The master is not the one who does not feel pride.
He is the one who feels it rise and chooses to set it down.

Ego is subtle in its corrosion.
It turns leadership into dominance.
It turns service into performance.
It turns endurance into display.

When ego takes root, power ceases to be a burden carried for others.
It becomes a mirror, reflecting the self back endlessly —
magnified, distorted, fragile.

The Shifu understands that power must remain impersonal.
It cannot be welded to the ego or it will warp.
It must be carried carefully, like a blade without a handle —
powerful, but dangerous to the one who clutches it too tightly.

The undisciplined mind believes it can master ego by suppressing it, by denying it exists.
But the disciplined mind knows better.
Ego is not erased.
It is managed.

Each day it must be recognized and set aside.
Each victory must be accepted and released.
Each compliment must be heard and let go.

The practice never ends.
The corrosion never fully stops.
But the master endures it — not by defeating ego once, but by refusing to serve it every day.

Stillness is not the absence of ego.
It is the refusal to be moved by it.

The Shifu does not collapse under the weight of power because he does not allow ego to make the burden heavier than it already is. He moves through praise as he moves through criticism — carefully, steadily, without clinging.

Authority must not become identity.
Power must not become the self.

The discipline endures only when the self is quiet enough to carry it without collapse.

Leading Without Owning

Leadership is not possession.
It is stewardship.

The world teaches that to lead is to own — to hold the title, the influence, the results.
But this belief corrupts the nature of leadership from the beginning.
It turns service into dominion.
It turns responsibility into control.
It turns the path into property.

The Shifu knows that true leadership demands the opposite.
It demands the willingness to guide without owning, to build

without attaching, to serve without branding the work with one's name.

What is built must not be bound.
What is guided must not be held.

Shaolin teaches that the master is not the one who accumulates followers.
He is the one who prepares others to walk without him.
His success is measured not in how many depend on him, but in how many can endure without him.

To lead without owning is to hold the work lightly, but with care — as one holds a vessel made of clay, knowing that grasping too tightly will break it, and holding too loosely will drop it.

It is to act not for affirmation, but for the sake of the work itself.
To make decisions not to preserve status, but to protect the path.
To step back when stepping back is what service demands, even when stepping forward would bring applause.

The undisciplined mind craves possession.
It needs to be seen as the architect, the founder, the indispensable center.
But the master knows better.
He understands that the highest leadership is invisible.
It leaves no trace except in the quiet endurance of what was built.

He does not sign his name where none is needed.
He does not bind the work to himself.
He builds carefully, quietly, then steps aside — allowing the work to breathe, to grow, to endure on its own.

Ownership is a weight the Shifu refuses to carry.
It is a temptation he sets down each time it rises.

Stillness teaches that the breath belongs to no one.
The work is the same.

To lead without owning is to serve without self.
It is to build what endures, not what flatters.

Authority is not an inheritance to be claimed.
It is a trust to be honored, then released.

The Shifu moves through leadership as he moves through the world —
anchored, careful, unattached.

And when he is no longer needed,
he disappears without noise,
leaving behind not a monument, but a way.

Chapter 19:

Violence Without Violence

The Illusion of Force

Force is not strength.
It is the appearance of strength.

It is easy to confuse violence with power, to believe that the one
who strikes first, who speaks loudest, who moves with
aggression, holds the advantage.
But Shaolin discipline teaches otherwise.
It teaches that true power is not measured by the ability to
destroy, but by the ability to choose not to.

The untrained mind believes that violence wins because it ends
resistance.
But what violence often ends is not resistance — it is dialogue,
possibility, relationship.
It leaves victory hollow and survival bitter.

Force demands reaction.
It seeks to provoke fear, to bend others through threat, to establish
dominance.
But dominance is fragile.
It lasts only as long as the strength to enforce it remains.
It breeds resentment beneath obedience, rebellion beneath silence.

The Shifu understands that violence is a trap.
It draws the mind into thinking that speed and aggression are the measures of mastery, when they are often the signs of panic, of a lack of control.

Shaolin forms are built not only to strike but to avoid striking — to redirect, to absorb, to allow the force of the opponent to exhaust itself without meeting it head-on.

The river does not break the rock by attacking it.
It wears it down by patience, by flowing where the rock cannot move.

The master does not fear the use of force.
He prepares for it, trains for it, accepts that there may be moments when it must be applied.
But he never confuses the ability to strike with the necessity of striking.

To move first is not always to win.
To hit harder is not always to prevail.

Real strength is seen in the refusal to strike without necessity — in the calm restraint of the hand that could, but chooses not to.

Violence is a temptation precisely because it is immediate.
It offers a solution that feels powerful.
But the solutions that endure are not built on fear.
They are built on patience, on clarity, on the quiet understanding that power exercised in restraint lasts longer than power exercised in rage.

The illusion of force is that it can solve what only endurance can survive.

The Shifu who has mastered himself does not rush to violence because he knows that to defeat an opponent is not the same as to prevail over a situation.

Victory by destruction is easy.
Victory by endurance is mastery.

To act without needing to break.
To defend without needing to destroy.
To endure without needing to retaliate.

This is strength beyond force —
and the only strength that does not collapse when the fight is over.

The Discipline of Restraint

Restraint is not weakness.
It is discipline under pressure.

The world misunderstands restraint.
It sees the one who holds back as fearful, uncertain, lesser.
But to those who walk the path of endurance, restraint is not the absence of strength — it is its highest refinement.

Shaolin teaches that the strongest form is the one that holds energy without spilling it.
The greatest punch is the one that remains unthrown, stored in the body like a coiled spring, present but contained.

To strike is easy.
It is immediate, reactive, satisfying.

But to restrain the hand, to quiet the breath, to hold the stance without unleashing it — this is mastery.

The undisciplined mind believes that to act is to prove strength. The disciplined mind knows that to not act — when action would be easy and destructive — is a deeper power.

Restraint demands more than control of the body.
It demands control of the ego — the part that demands to be seen, to be heard, to be feared.
It demands mastery over the instinct that equates action with worth, violence with victory.

The Shifu does not withhold action because he is unsure.
He withholds it because he is sure — sure that not all battles are worthy, that not all provocations deserve response, that not all threats require destruction.

Restraint is not a performance.
It is not a pose held for others to admire.
It is a private discipline, invisible to those who believe that noise and motion are proofs of life.

In restraint, the master preserves not only himself but the field itself —
refusing to escalate conflict, refusing to leave scars that cannot be undone, refusing to create enemies where patience could have built allies.

The river does not resist the stone by attacking it.
It resists by flowing around it, over it, beyond it — enduring longer than the stone can hold.

Restraint is this quiet endurance.

It allows force to pass without becoming force itself.
It accepts the tension of holding potential energy without needing to unleash it.

The undisciplined mind craves release.
It wants the satisfaction of the blow struck, the anger voiced, the dominance proven.
But the master remains still — not because he cannot act, but because he knows he must not.

Restraint is the discipline that endures when strength alone would fail.
It is the shield that protects not only the self but the path, the work, the future that violence would shatter.

To act without thought is instinct.
To withhold action without cowardice is mastery.

The Shifu who has trained restraint does not fear his power.
He fears what would happen if he forgot when to withhold it.

In restraint, he holds not only his hand —
he holds the breath, the mind, the path itself — steady, unbroken, alive.

Winning Without Harm

Victory is often imagined as the defeat of the opponent, the destruction of resistance, the silencing of opposition.

But this vision of victory is shallow.
It is loud, immediate, and ultimately fragile.

The Shifu knows that the highest victory is not to destroy, but to prevail without harm.
To resolve conflict without violence.
To maintain presence without forcing submission.
To end the struggle without leaving wounds that will fester and grow.

Winning without harm is not a matter of avoiding conflict at any cost.
It is a matter of moving through conflict without letting it dictate the terms of engagement.

In Shaolin practice, every movement has its counter — not to clash with force, but to redirect it, to absorb and release it, to let the aggression exhaust itself without finding an anchor in you.

The master wins by refusing to escalate.
By absorbing the energy directed at him and offering nothing back that would inflame it.
By stepping aside without surrender, by standing firm without provoking.

This is not passivity.
It is not avoidance.

It is the deliberate choice to act with discipline rather than impulse, to move carefully rather than react blindly.

The undisciplined seek to win by domination.
The master seeks to win by resolution.

Victory achieved through destruction leaves scars that require generations to heal.

Victory achieved through endurance leaves no scar at all — only the quiet absence of further conflict.

The river does not destroy the stone by force.
It wears it down by persistence, by gentleness, by movement that never ceases and never needs to shout.

So too does the Shifu endure aggression without becoming aggression.

He steps when he must, acts when necessary, but never beyond what the moment requires.

He does not fight to defeat the opponent.
He moves to preserve the breath, the path, the way forward.

The highest victory is not the silencing of the enemy, but the silencing of conflict itself.

To prevail without harm is to understand that the true opponent is not the one who stands before you.
It is the collapse of discipline, the surrender to ego, the abandonment of stillness.

The Shifu who wins without harm has not merely ended the conflict.
He has preserved the work, the self, the way — intact.

Victory without harm is quiet.
It is often unseen.
But it endures longer than any triumph gained by force.

The master does not need to be celebrated.
He does not need to be feared.
He needs only to remain —
whole, quiet, disciplined —
when the storm has passed.

This is winning without harm:
to stand, to endure, to prevail —
without leaving behind anything that must later be undone.

Chapter 20:

Betrayal Without Bitterness

Trust Is Risk

Trust is not a guarantee.
It is a risk.

Every relationship, every alliance, every bond we form is an
opening — a gate through which both loyalty and betrayal can
pass.
To trust is to accept that risk — not blindly, but willingly, with
full knowledge that betrayal is not just possible, but inevitable in
some form over the course of a life.

The undisciplined mind seeks certainty.
It demands assurances that cannot be given, guarantees that
cannot be enforced.
It imagines trust as a shield against hurt, a contract against
betrayal.

But trust is no shield.
It is a choice to remain open in a world where openness can
wound.

Shaolin discipline does not teach the practitioner to close
themselves to others in the name of safety.
It teaches the opposite:
to remain open, even knowing the cost.

Trust is risk — but it is a necessary risk.

To lead, to build, to endure — all of these demand connection. And connection demands trust.

The Shifu knows that trust will be broken.
Not always with malice.
Sometimes with carelessness, sometimes with fear, sometimes simply because the burdens of the path grow too heavy for those who once promised to walk it beside you.

He does not expect betrayal, but neither is he surprised by it.

Trust is a risk — but one worth taking.

To close oneself entirely is to forfeit the deeper work.
It is to live not in stillness, but in suspicion.
It is to mistake isolation for invulnerability.

The master trusts because trust is necessary for the work to endure.
He accepts the possibility of betrayal without bitterness, because he understands that the alternative — a life closed off, unreachable, disconnected — is a slower, deeper collapse.

The river does not flow only where the ground is certain.
It flows where it must, even over stones that will one day shift beneath it.

Trust is this flow — knowing the ground may move, but moving anyway.

The Shifu does not demand certainty before trusting.
He does not require proof before extending his hand.
He trusts not because he is naïve, but because he is disciplined enough to endure what may come.

Trust is not foolishness.
It is not weakness.
It is the strength to accept risk without collapsing into fear.

The betrayal, when it comes, is not the end of trust.
It is merely a test of whether trust was ever real —
whether it was strong enough to survive the breaking,
quiet enough to continue without bitterness.

Trust is risk.
The master accepts it — fully, without defense —
and continues.

Endurance Over Injury

Betrayal is a wound no armor can prevent.
It cuts not the body, but the breath — reaching inward, striking
the places most carefully protected.

There is no discipline strong enough to erase the pain of betrayal.
Even the master feels the sting, the hollow ache where trust once
lived.

But endurance does not require the absence of pain.
It requires the refusal to be undone by it.

The undisciplined mind collapses under betrayal.
It turns inward, closing doors that once stood open.
It hardens into suspicion, into resentment, into a life smaller and
more guarded than before.

But the Shifu endures the injury differently.

He does not pretend he has not been wounded.
He does not deny the loss, the disappointment, the quiet anger
that betrayal awakens.

He allows himself to feel these things — not because he is weak,
but because he is strong enough to face the truth of them without
being ruled by them.

Endurance over injury is not numbness.
It is not forgetting.

It is remembering without allowing memory to turn into poison.
It is carrying the wound without letting it define the self.

Shaolin teaches that injury is inevitable in practice.
There is no mastery without strain, without bruises, without falls.

But the body heals — not by erasing the injury, but by growing
stronger around it.

The spirit heals in the same way.

The betrayal remains.
The scar remains.
But the Shifu does not allow it to harden into bitterness.

He does not abandon trust because it has been broken once, or
many times.
He does not let injury close the gate he has worked so long to
keep open.

Endurance is not survival alone.
It is survival without corruption.

The river continues its course even when rocks divert it, even
when landslides narrow its path.

It does not abandon its source.
It adjusts.
It endures.

The Shifu moves forward —
wounded, perhaps slower for a time, but still moving, still
breathing, still open.

He refuses to let injury have the final word.
He refuses to let betrayal become the architect of his future.

Endurance over injury is the quiet decision to live fully even
when others have failed you.
To trust again, not blindly, but bravely.
To carry the wound, but not to let the wound carry you.

The master endures not because he is untouched,
but because he knows that to stop moving is to surrender the
discipline he has spent a lifetime building.

He endures because the breath continues.
Because the path demands it.
Because the self — if it is to remain whole — must refuse to
collapse.

Forward Without Closure

Closure is a comfort the world promises but rarely delivers.
It is the hope that every wound will be explained, every betrayal

confessed, every hurt acknowledged and made clean by apology or justice.

But the Shifu knows better.

He understands that closure is not a guarantee.
It is not even a necessity.

Life does not tie itself into neat endings.
Betrayals are often left unresolved — the apologies never given, the wrongs never righted, the reasons never fully explained.
The one who waits for closure waits in vain.

The undisciplined mind demands closure before it moves.
It insists that peace can only be found when the wound has been acknowledged, when the score has been settled.

But this is a trap.
It turns pain into permanence.
It binds the self to the injury, making forward movement conditional on the actions of others.

The Shifu does not wait.
He does not demand what cannot be given.
He does not surrender his breath, his path, his endurance to the failings of others.

He moves forward without closure —
not because he is indifferent, but because he is disciplined.

Shaolin practice teaches that the opponent does not have to acknowledge defeat for the master to prevail.
Victory is not external.
It is internal — the preservation of stillness, the refusal to collapse.

Closure is an illusion of control.
The belief that the past can be repaired, that the pain can be undone.

But discipline teaches acceptance —
not of the betrayal itself, but of the reality that some wounds will remain open.
Some wrongs will remain unanswered.

Stillness does not come from resolution.
It comes from refusal — refusal to let the past dictate the breath, the step, the way forward.

The river does not wait for the mountain to apologize for standing in its path.
It flows — around, beyond, onward.

So too must the Shifu move.

Forward — carrying the weight, but not allowing the weight to dictate the movement.
Forward — breathing the same breath, even if it carries sorrow within it.
Forward — not because the past is clean, but because the present demands endurance.

Closure may never come.
Peace may never be complete.

But movement is still possible.
Presence is still possible.
Endurance is still possible.

The master does not wait for the world to make things right.
He moves because the breath continues.
Because stillness must be preserved.

Because to wait is to surrender the discipline that gives life its true shape.

Forward — without closure.
Forward — without bitterness.

Forward — because there is no other way.

Chapter 21:

Isolation Without Collapse

Leadership Is Isolation

Leadership is not companionship.
It is not comfort.
It is not a place where belonging is guaranteed.

Leadership, in its true form, is isolation.

The Shifu knows this.
He accepts that to lead is to stand apart — not because he desires separation, but because the work demands it.

The world misunderstands leadership.
It imagines the leader at the center of adoration, surrounded by loyalty, propped up by admiration.
But real leadership strips these illusions away.

True leadership is silent responsibility.
It is the weight of decisions carried alone.
It is the burden of clarity when others prefer confusion.
It is the endurance of standing firm when others have drifted or fled.

The higher the view, the thinner the air.

The higher the responsibility, the fewer who can share it.

The master understands that to lead is to accept this solitude —
not with bitterness, not with pride, but with quiet endurance.

Isolation in leadership is not merely physical separation.
It is the deeper solitude of the spirit — the knowledge that final
decisions cannot be shared, that final accountability cannot be
passed to another.

It is the silence that comes when the path forward is unclear and
the burden of choosing rests solely on your shoulders.
It is the stillness that follows when you speak a hard truth and
find no one standing beside you.

The undisciplined mind seeks leadership for its rewards — the
titles, the respect, the visible stature.
But these are hollow consolations when the true cost becomes
clear.

The Shifu does not seek to escape isolation.
He accepts it as the shape of real leadership.
He does not expect to be understood at every step.
He does not expect to be supported at every moment.

Shaolin discipline teaches that the practitioner trains alone even in
a crowded hall.
The forms are learned side by side, but mastery is individual —
earned in the silence between the breaths, in the unshared struggle
of repetition.

So it is with leadership.

The Shifu stands — not because he is surrounded, but because he
is anchored.
Not because he is carried by others, but because he carries the
path itself.

Leadership is isolation.
Not a flaw.
Not a punishment.
A reality — to be accepted, endured, and carried without collapse.

The master walks forward alone —
not because he desires solitude,
but because the work demands the strength to endure it.

Solitude as Forge

Solitude, properly understood, is not an absence.
It is a forge.

It is the place where strength is refined beyond the reach of
applause, where clarity is honed in the silence left when external
validation fades.

The Shifu does not seek solitude as escape.
He accepts it as necessity — the necessary fire through which
presence must pass if it is to endure without collapse.

Shaolin discipline teaches that endurance is not built under the
eyes of others.
It is built alone, in the moments unseen — in the early hours, in
the quiet practice, in the repetition that no one applauds and few
would endure.

So it is with leadership.

The solitude that comes with leadership is not punishment.
It is the place where the self is tempered — stripped of the need for approval, hardened against the erosion of doubt, sharpened against the softening effect of praise.

In solitude, the leader faces himself — not as he wishes to be seen, but as he truly is.
There is no audience, no mirror, no stage.
Only the breath, the body, the mind — and the weight they must carry together.

The undisciplined mind seeks to avoid solitude.
It fears the silence, the absence of affirmation, the confrontation with the unadorned self.

But the disciplined mind steps into solitude willingly, understanding that only in isolation can the noise be quieted, only there can the root be tested and found sound.

Solitude is a forge because it reveals weakness not to shame but to strengthen.
It burns away illusion.
It removes the crutches of external validation.
It leaves only what is real — breath, discipline, endurance.

The Shifu accepts solitude not because he enjoys it, but because he knows he cannot complete the path without it.

The river is not shaped by crowds.
It is shaped by the lonely persistence of water against stone, day after day, unseen.

The leader is not shaped by followers.
He is shaped by the endurance built in the moments when no one is watching, when the burden feels too heavy, when the way forward is unclear and the only answer is to continue.

Solitude is not an enemy.
It is a forge.

And the Shifu steps into it not because it is easy,
but because it is necessary.

Remaining Whole Alone

To be alone is not to be broken.
To be alone is to be whole without the scaffolding of others.

The undisciplined spirit fractures in isolation.
It was never whole to begin with.
It leaned on admiration, on agreement, on applause.
When these vanish, the self collapses — not because of isolation,
but because there was no true self there to sustain it.

The Shifu knows that leadership requires the ability to remain
whole even when the circle thins, even when the crowds disperse,
even when the voices that once cheered fall silent.

Stillness is not the absence of company.
It is the presence of an unshaken self.

To remain whole alone is not to become cold or indifferent.
It is not the denial of connection or the rejection of community.
It is the quiet endurance of the self — intact, undiminished —
even when support is absent.

It is the ability to carry responsibility when others walk away.
It is the patience to hold to the path when others forget it.

It is the strength to keep moving when others cannot or will not continue.

Shaolin practice teaches that the stance must be able to hold under pressure — not just for moments, but for hours if needed.
The body must find its own center.
The mind must settle into its own breath.

So too with leadership.

The Shifu stands not because he is carried by the energy of others, but because he carries his own stillness, his own breath, his own center.

Isolation reveals the true weight of leadership:
to carry not just the work, but the quiet endurance required to sustain it through the silence, through the loneliness, through the unseen seasons of labor.

The river flows not because it is seen, but because it must.
The master moves forward not because he is celebrated, but because the work demands continuation.

Remaining whole alone is not a performance.
It is not a shield against sorrow.
It is a discipline — the breath drawn not for applause, but for survival.
The step taken not for recognition, but because the way remains.

The Shifu does not collapse in isolation.
He endures it.
He accepts it.
He carries it — carefully, quietly — until it is no longer a burden, but simply a part of the path.

To remain whole alone is to remain whole always.

Stillness is not dependent.
Presence is not conditional.
The breath continues — whether watched or unseen.

And the master stands —
intact, unbroken —
even when he stands alone.

Chapter 22:

Certainty Without Arrogance

The Danger of Being Right

Certainty is a quiet force.
When shaped by discipline, it becomes a steady anchor.
When corrupted by ego, it becomes a silent destroyer.

The danger of being right is not in the truth itself, but in what
certainty invites:
pride, superiority, the slow erosion of humility.

The undisciplined mind craves certainty not as a foundation, but
as a weapon.
It seeks to wield correctness over others, to silence dissent, to
impose itself through knowledge rather than presence.

But the Shifu understands that truth is not a bludgeon.
It is a path — narrow, shifting, demanding care.

To be right is a quiet responsibility.
It demands patience.
It demands restraint.
It demands the humility to know that being right is not the same
as being beyond error.

Shaolin practice teaches that the master does not stop practicing
because his form is correct.

He continues — correcting, refining, adjusting — because perfection is not a state but a practice.

So it is with certainty.

The disciplined mind holds truth carefully, aware of its weight, aware of its fragility.
It understands that even the clearest insight must be handled with humility, or it becomes arrogance.

Certainty without humility blinds.
It closes the mind.
It builds walls around the self, walls so high that no new understanding can enter.

The Shifu knows that truth held arrogantly becomes brittle.
It cannot bend.
It cannot endure.

Real certainty is flexible — strong, but not rigid.
It endures challenge not by resisting it blindly, but by engaging it carefully, seeing in every opposition not an attack but an invitation to deeper understanding.

To be right is to be responsible for how truth is carried.
It is to remember that even the clearest water grows stagnant when it does not flow.

Certainty must move.
It must remain alive, humble, open — or it hardens into self-righteousness, the dead form of what once was living understanding.

The river does not boast that it reaches the sea.
It simply moves, bends, flows — certain of its direction, but never stiff in its course.

So too must the Shifu carry certainty.

Not as a badge.
Not as a sword.
But as a responsibility — quiet, steady, and always alive to the possibility that even what seems clear today may demand a deeper seeing tomorrow.

The danger of being right is the temptation to believe the work is done.

But the breath continues.
The practice continues.
And certainty, if it is to endure, must be carried carefully — never with arrogance,
always with humility.

Conviction Without Closing

Conviction is not the enemy of growth.
But when held too tightly, it becomes a gate locked from the inside.

The undisciplined spirit mistakes conviction for completion.
It believes that to be certain is to have arrived, to have no further need of questioning, of adjusting, of learning.

But the Shifu knows better.

Conviction, properly understood, is not a closing.
It is a commitment — to the path, not to a fixed position on it.

Shaolin practice teaches that even the deepest stance must remain alive.
The knees bent, the breath fluid, the body ready to adjust with the shifting of weight, the movement of force.

Stillness, too, is alive.
It is not frozen.
It breathes.

Conviction must be the same — anchored but breathing, steady but flexible.

The mind that closes around certainty hardens.
It becomes brittle, unable to absorb new truth, unable to adjust to shifting conditions.
It mistakes rigidity for strength, stubbornness for resilience.

The Shifu carries conviction as he carries the breath —
not held so tightly that it cannot expand,
not so loosely that it dissipates.

He understands that the path demands steadiness — but also openness.
The willingness to be wrong.
The humility to relearn.
The discipline to refine.

Conviction without closing is the discipline of holding to one's root without abandoning the possibility of deeper understanding.
It is the willingness to listen even while standing firm.
It is the ability to absorb without surrendering, to adjust without losing center.

The river, though certain of its movement toward the sea, bends with the land.
It shifts course when the terrain demands it.

It does not abandon its source or its destination, but it adjusts its path without hesitation.

So must conviction flow.

The master holds conviction not as a shield against change, but as a guide through it.
He stands — but he stands alive, breathing, seeing.
He moves — but he moves without panic, without the need to defend the self at every turn.

Conviction must not close the mind.
It must anchor it — steady enough to resist collapse, open enough to allow growth.

The Shifu remains faithful to the breath, to the discipline, to the path —
not by freezing, but by flowing,
not by locking down, but by standing firm in a way that still allows motion.

Conviction without closing is strength without arrogance.
Presence without rigidity.
Certainty without blindness.

It is the breath drawn fully —
and released without fear.

Truth Held Lightly

Truth is not a weapon to be wielded heavily.
It is a thread to be carried lightly — with care, with humility, with endurance.

The undisciplined spirit grips truth too tightly.
It clutches at certainties as if they could shield against the discomfort of change, the uncertainty of life, the inevitability of being wrong.

But truth held too tightly suffocates.
It hardens the mind, closes the heart, blinds the vision.

The Shifu knows that truth must be carried as one carries water in the hand — not clenched, but cradled.
Too tight, and it spills.
Too loose, and it slips away.

Shaolin discipline teaches that the practitioner must remain alive to correction — that the perfect form is not fixed, but dynamic, adjusting breath by breath, moment by moment.

So it is with truth.

Truth held lightly remains alive.
It remains flexible.
It allows for nuance, for complexity, for the humility to admit that deeper truths may lie beyond what is now seen.

To hold truth lightly is not to treat it as unimportant.
It is to recognize its living nature — its demand for care rather than conquest.

The river, sure of its destination, carries its waters lightly.
It does not freeze into hardness.
It moves, breathes, bends — certain of its source, certain of its
direction, but never rigid.

The Shifu moves the same way.

He holds truth with seriousness, but without arrogance.
He speaks carefully, knowing that even the clearest insights must
be offered without the weight of self-importance.
He listens carefully, understanding that even disagreement can
reveal edges of the truth he has not yet seen.

Truth, when held lightly, becomes a guide, not a prison.
It invites others to walk alongside, not to kneel before.
It opens the mind rather than closing it.

The master does not wield truth as a hammer.
He carries it as a light — steady, quiet, enduring.

To hold truth lightly is to remain in motion.
It is to allow the breath to continue, the learning to continue, the
way to remain open.

The undisciplined mind seeks to possess truth.
The disciplined mind seeks to serve it — carefully, patiently,
without clenching.

The Shifu knows that the discipline of truth is not in holding
tighter.
It is in holding better.

Truth held lightly endures.
It moves without losing form.
It breathes without losing strength.

It is the way of the breath —
steady, quiet, alive.

And the master, breathing with it,
remains —
anchored, enduring, free.

Chapter 23:

Doubt Without Abandonment

Doubt Is a Companion

Doubt is not the enemy of the path.
It is its companion.

To walk without doubt is not mastery.
It is delusion.

The undisciplined spirit believes that certainty must be complete, unbroken, unwavering.
It imagines that the master feels no hesitation, no questioning, no inner unrest.
But this is a misunderstanding of the nature of the way.

Doubt is not a sign of weakness.
It is a sign that the mind remains alive, that the heart remains honest, that the self remains humble before the vastness of the unknown.

The Shifu does not fear doubt.
He accepts it as part of the journey — not a defect, but a signal.
A signal that the breath must be drawn deeper, that the stance must be held steadier, that the attention must sharpen.

Shaolin discipline teaches that balance is not the absence of sway, but the continual correction of sway.
So it is with certainty.

Certainty without doubt hardens into arrogance.
It blinds the eyes and deafens the ears.
It closes the mind to what lies just beyond the edges of comfort.

But doubt, carried properly, humbles without paralyzing.
It softens the mind without dissolving the will.
It sharpens the questions without eroding the foundation.

The Shifu does not allow doubt to command him.
But neither does he attempt to silence it.

He listens.
He questions.
He adjusts — carefully, deliberately — always returning to the breath, to the root, to the discipline that endures even when the mind trembles.

Doubt is a companion, not a master.

It walks beside the Shifu — a reminder that the way is not owned, that the work is not complete, that mastery is a path, not a possession.

The river, sure of its direction, does not rush blindly.
It bends, it hesitates, it pools in stillness before moving on.
It doubts, not its destination, but its route.

The master doubts in the same way.

He does not doubt the breath.
He does not doubt the value of stillness.
But he doubts his own clarity.

He questions his own certainty.
And in doing so, he deepens his presence, sharpens his endurance.

Doubt is not a flaw to be eradicated.
It is a tool to be respected —
carried carefully,
listened to quietly,
set aside when it no longer serves.

The Shifu walks with doubt —
not as a burden,
but as a reminder.

The breath continues,
even when the way grows uncertain.
The discipline endures,
even when the mind wavers.

And the master moves forward —
not because doubt is absent,
but because doubt is understood.

Moving Without Guarantee

Movement is not the reward for certainty.
It is the discipline in its absence.

The undisciplined mind waits for the way to be clear, for all risks
to be measured, for all doubts to be resolved.
It believes that only when certainty is complete should the next

step be taken.
But this is a path that leads nowhere.

The Shifu knows that waiting for guarantees is a form of
surrender — not to wisdom, but to fear.
The way does not unfold only for those who demand certainty.
It reveals itself to those who are willing to move without it.

Shaolin practice teaches that the stance is not perfect before it is
practiced.
It is perfected in movement — breath by breath, adjustment by
adjustment, repetition after repetition.

So it is with the journey.

Clarity is not a precondition.
It is a companion discovered along the way — fleeting, imperfect,
deepening only through persistence.

To move without guarantee is not recklessness.
It is discipline.
It is the quiet decision to act carefully, deliberately, even when
outcomes are unclear and the path is shadowed by doubt.

The river does not know what stones lie ahead.
It moves anyway, adjusting its flow, shifting its current, remaining
faithful to its source and its destination without knowing the
shape of every turn.

The master moves the same way.

He does not demand assurance before acting.
He does not wait for perfect understanding before stepping.
He breathes.
He moves.

He endures — adjusting where needed, holding course where possible, accepting uncertainty without surrendering the way.

To move without guarantee is to trust the discipline, not the conditions.
It is to remain faithful to the breath, even when the air is thin.
It is to act not because success is assured, but because the next step is necessary.

The undisciplined spirit confuses caution with paralysis.
It waits so long for certainty that it abandons the work before it begins.

The Shifu does not wait.

He carries doubt carefully.
He listens to it.
But he does not serve it.

He moves —
not because the ground is firm,
but because the breath continues.
Not because the outcome is clear,
but because the path demands it.

Movement is not the sign of certainty.
It is the proof of discipline.

The master steps forward —
not recklessly,
not blindly,
but steadily —
carrying his doubt with him,
and moving anyway.

Faith Without Evidence

Faith, properly understood, is not belief without questioning.
It is endurance without proof.

The undisciplined spirit believes that faith must be propped up by
evidence — by signs, by reassurances, by visible progress.
Without these, it collapses, mistaking uncertainty for failure.

But the Shifu knows that real faith begins where evidence ends.
It is the quiet trust that the breath continues even when the wind
rises.
It is the steady movement forward even when the path disappears
into mist.

Shaolin discipline teaches that the practitioner must trust the
process long before results appear.
That the form must be practiced, the stance held, the breath drawn
— not because mastery is guaranteed, but because mastery is
impossible without persistence through uncertainty.

Faith is this persistence.

It is not blindness.
It is not denial of difficulty.
It is the choice to continue when the mind demands clarity, when
the heart demands ease, when the world offers neither.

Faith without evidence is not foolishness.
It is discipline made visible.

It is the breath drawn fully even when the outcome remains
hidden.
It is the step taken carefully even when the destination is

unknown.
It is the work carried forward not because it is affirmed, but because it is necessary.

The river does not see the sea from its source.
It moves anyway, trusting its course, guided not by sight but by deeper forces, invisible yet enduring.

The Shifu moves the same way.

He does not wait for signs to continue.
He does not demand reassurance before he breathes again.
He trusts the path — not because he has seen its end, but because he has committed to the way.

Faith without evidence is the discipline to build without applause, to endure without guarantee, to carry the work forward even when the world falls silent.

It is the breath taken in darkness.
It is the stance held in silence.
It is the endurance that remains not because the way is easy, but because the way is worthy.

The undisciplined mind demands to see before it believes.
The master believes —
not because he sees,
but because he breathes.

Faith is not the absence of doubt.
It is the refusal to be ruled by it.

The Shifu carries his breath, his discipline, his endurance —
not because the evidence is clear,
but because the way endures beyond the reach of evidence.

Faith without evidence.
Movement without assurance.
Stillness without certainty.

This is the way of the master.

This is the breath that continues.

Chapter 24:

Fear Without Paralysis

Fear Is the Breath Quickened

Fear is not an intruder.
It is a companion — a natural and inevitable part of movement, of risk, of life.

The undisciplined mind treats fear as failure, as evidence that something is wrong, that the path should be abandoned.
But the Shifu understands that fear is not the signal to stop.
It is the breath quickened, the senses sharpened, the mind awakened.

Fear is not weakness.
It is awareness heightened by the weight of consequence.

Shaolin discipline teaches that the breath must remain steady even as the heart pounds, even as the muscles tense, even as the body prepares for what cannot be fully controlled.
The breath does not erase fear.
It carries it.

To feel fear is to be alive to risk, to danger, to uncertainty.
It is not the presence of fear that marks the difference between the master and the novice.
It is what is done with that fear.

The undisciplined spirit collapses into fear, allowing it to dictate action — or worse, inaction.
It hesitates when movement is necessary.
It freezes when breath must continue.

But the Shifu does not deny fear.
He acknowledges it, feels it fully, but refuses to be ruled by it.

Fear quickens the breath.
The master slows it.
Fear tightens the muscles.
The master relaxes into the tension.

To breathe within fear is to remain present.
It is to allow fear its place — but not its command.

The river does not stop flowing when the rains make it violent.
It does not fight the current.
It moves — faster, perhaps harder — but it moves.

So too must the Shifu move with fear —
not against it, not through denial of it —
but with it, carefully, steadily, without collapse.

Fear is not the signal to abandon the path.
It is the reminder that the stakes are real, that the breath must be drawn deeper, that the movement must be made more carefully.

The master carries fear —
not as a burden, but as a part of the journey.

He feels the quickening of the breath.
He slows it deliberately.
He feels the trembling in the body.
He steadies it carefully.

Fear does not disappear.
It is endured —
not by force,
but by discipline.

Stillness within fear.
Breath within fear.
Movement within fear.

This is the way of the master.
This is the breath that continues.

Endurance Through Fear

Endurance is not the absence of fear.
It is the decision to continue moving through it.

The undisciplined spirit waits for fear to vanish before acting.
It imagines that courage is the elimination of fear, that mastery is
the absence of trembling, hesitation, doubt.
But fear never disappears fully.
It only changes shape.

The Shifu understands that fear is not an obstacle to be
conquered, but a reality to be endured.
It is not an enemy to be destroyed, but a companion to be carried.

Shaolin discipline teaches that the breath must remain even when
the body is strained, even when exhaustion makes stillness feel
impossible.

The discipline is not in the ease of the breath.
It is in its continuation — strained, shallow, but unbroken.

So it is with fear.

Endurance is not grace under pressure.
It is breath under pressure.
It is movement without collapse, even when the ground feels
unstable, even when the heart beats too fast, even when the mind
demands retreat.

Fear makes the path heavier.
But the master does not set the weight down.
He adjusts his stance.
He shortens his steps.
He draws the breath deeper.
He continues.

The river narrows between stone walls.
It rages faster, its surface broken, its depth tested.
But it does not abandon its course.

The Shifu endures fear in the same way —
allowing the quickened breath, the tightened chest, the trembling
hands —
but refusing to halt, to surrender, to retreat.

The undisciplined mind believes that fear is a signal to stop.
The disciplined mind knows that fear is a signal to steady.

To endure through fear is to recognize its voice without obeying
it.
It is to accept its presence without submitting to its demand for
paralysis.

The Shifu moves not because fear has been silenced, but because he has learned to breathe louder than fear whispers.

He acts — carefully, patiently, steadily —
not because fear has disappeared,
but because stillness has been built to endure it.

Fear will accompany every real movement, every serious work,
every necessary risk.
It cannot be removed.
It can only be carried.

And the master carries it —
quietly, steadily —
through the trembling,
through the uncertainty,
through the doubt.

Endurance is not fearlessness.
It is faithful breath drawn in the presence of fear.

The way continues —
not in spite of fear,
but alongside it.

Stillness Beyond Terror

Terror is fear magnified — sharpened, deepened, overwhelming.
It is the point where fear ceases to whisper and begins to shout.

The undisciplined mind collapses in terror.
It rushes for escape, abandons the breath, surrenders the center.
It believes that stillness is impossible when the heart races, when the body shakes, when the mind is flooded with visions of failure, of loss, of harm.

But the Shifu knows otherwise.

Stillness is not the absence of terror.
It is presence beyond it.

Shaolin teaches that in the moment of deepest strain — when the body screams to stop, when the muscles tremble past control — the breath must remain.
Not perfect.
Not calm.
Present.

Terror cannot be erased.
It can only be endured.
Stillness is not about silencing the terror.
It is about refusing to be moved by it.

The river, in flood, rages.
Its surface broken, its course violent.
But beneath the turbulence, the deeper currents remain steady, slow, unhurried.

So too does the Shifu remain beneath terror —
the breath drawn slowly,
the body grounded carefully,
the mind refusing to shatter even as it trembles.

Stillness beyond terror is not a hero's courage.
It is not the absence of fear.

It is the mastery of breath when the body and mind demand collapse.

It is endurance at its deepest.
The refusal to run.
The refusal to collapse.
The refusal to abandon the self in the moment when the self is most tempted to break apart.

The undisciplined mind believes that terror must be defeated.
The disciplined mind knows that terror must be endured.

Stillness in terror is quiet.
It is not dramatic.
It is not visible.
It is the simple, profound decision to remain —
to breathe, to stand, to endure —
even as every instinct pleads for surrender.

The Shifu does not escape terror.
He passes through it.

He feels its weight.
He accepts its presence.
And he draws the next breath — not easily, not without trembling
— but steadily, patiently, faithfully.

Stillness is not a victory over fear.
It is presence within it.

The breath continues.
The stance holds.
The path remains.

Beyond terror, there is no certainty, no ease —
only the breath, the step, the endurance.

And the master carries them —
carefully, quietly —
through the storm,
through the trembling,
through the fear.

Stillness beyond terror is the final proof of endurance.
It is the breath that refuses to abandon itself.

Chapter 25:

Disappearance Without Loss

The Master Fades

The true master is not marked by how he appears,
but by how he disappears.

The undisciplined spirit clings to recognition.
It seeks to leave behind monuments, titles, names engraved in
stone — something to prove it was here, something to resist the
pull of time.

But the Shifu understands that mastery is not proven by
permanence.
It is proven by the willingness to let go — to fade quietly,
carefully, without struggle, without noise.

Shaolin discipline teaches that true strength leaves no scar.
The perfect strike is the one that leaves no trace beyond its
necessity.
The perfect movement is the one forgotten the moment it is
completed.

So it is with the master.

He does not demand to be remembered.
He does not insist on being seen.

He builds carefully, endures patiently, leads quietly — and then steps away.

To disappear is not to be erased.
It is to allow the work to stand without leaning on the presence of its maker.

The river flows, carving the land, nourishing the valley — and moves on.
It leaves behind no statues to itself, only the shape of what it has touched.

The Shifu does the same.

He fades not because he has failed, but because he has succeeded.
He steps aside not because he is defeated, but because the work no longer needs his hand.
He disappears because the breath he carried has been passed on, quietly, without need for ceremony.

The undisciplined mind seeks applause in absence.
It wants to be missed, to be mourned, to be immortalized.

But the disciplined mind accepts that the highest work is that which can continue without its maker's presence.
The greatest leader is the one whose absence leaves not emptiness, but endurance.

Disappearance without loss is not a vanishing.
It is a completion — the quiet fulfillment of the path walked steadily and without collapse.

The Shifu fades not into nothingness, but into the breath of those who continue —
the presence he cultivated becoming part of the air around them, unseen, unclaimed.

True mastery is not clung to.
It is released —
with the same breath,
the same stillness,
the same discipline that built it.

The master fades.
And in fading, he endures.

Withdrawal as Completion

Withdrawal is not abandonment.
It is the final discipline.

The undisciplined spirit clings to the center.
It fears that stepping away will diminish its worth, erase its
contribution, undo its presence.
It imagines that to withdraw is to lose everything built.

But the Shifu knows that real completion is quiet.
It is the withdrawal that leaves no gap, only space — for the work
to breathe on its own, for others to stand without needing to be
held.

Shaolin practice teaches that the master does not remain on the
floor forever.
He trains the body, tempers the breath, strengthens the mind —
and then steps aside, leaving the student to stand alone.

Presence must not become dependency.
Leadership must not become possession.
Teaching must not become imprisonment.

The Shifu withdraws not because he is tired,
not because he is defeated,
not because he is no longer needed —
but because he has given what he came to give.

The withdrawal is not sudden.
It is not violent.
It is as patient as the building that preceded it — deliberate,
careful, breath by breath.

The undisciplined mind seeks to be remembered in withdrawal.
It lingers.
It haunts.
It leaves heavy footprints in the places it once stood.

But the master leaves lightly —
like the river receding after the flood,
like the wind after the storm,
like the hand withdrawing after the work is complete.

His mark is not in what remains of him.
It is in what endures without him.

Withdrawal as completion is the highest form of endurance.
It is the willingness to accept that the work is not yours to cling
to, but yours to carry carefully for a season —
and then to release.

The Shifu steps back without regret.
He disappears without noise.
He withdraws without resentment.

The work continues.
The breath continues.
The discipline continues.

And the master, unseen but present in what he leaves behind,
fades —
not into absence,
but into endurance.

The Quiet Exit

The exit of the master is not a ceremony.
It is a breath.

There is no announcement.
No proclamation.
No gathering to mark the moment.

The Shifu does not leave through a doorway.
He leaves through stillness —
a quiet shift, a subtle release, like a breath leaving the body
without sound.

The undisciplined spirit craves an ending filled with recognition,
a farewell that cements identity, a moment that validates all that
has been done.

But the master has no need for these things.
He knows that the highest departure is the one that leaves no scar,

no clinging,
no collapse.

Shaolin teaches that the highest movement is invisible —
not because it is hidden,
but because it is natural, inevitable, complete.

The master's exit is not a retreat.
It is not a defeat.
It is a continuation — of the breath, of the discipline, of the
endurance that was never his alone to carry.

He leaves no monument.
He leaves no shadow.

What he leaves is stronger than presence.
It is presence made independent.

The river does not announce when it changes course.
The wind does not declare when it shifts direction.

So too does the Shifu exit —
quietly, carefully, without demand, without disruption.

The undisciplined mind wants to be missed.
The disciplined mind wants only for the work to continue.

To exit quietly is to trust the work.
It is to believe that what was built has roots deeper than the
maker, breath longer than the builder, endurance stronger than the
leader.

The master's quiet exit is the final act of faith —
faith in the discipline,
faith in the way,
faith in the breath that continues beyond his presence.

There is no noise.
No fanfare.
Only the steady continuation of what matters most.

The Shifu fades.
And in fading,
he fulfills the path he walked from the beginning.

Stillness in movement.
Presence in absence.
Endurance without end.

The quiet exit leaves no mark.
And in leaving no mark,
it leaves everything.

Chapter 26:
Authority Without Ownership

Power Held Lightly

Power is weight.
Held too tightly, it crushes.
Held too loosely, it slips away.

The undisciplined mind clings to power.
It wraps itself around titles, influence, the outward signs of control.
It mistakes authority for identity.
It cannot imagine a self without command, without recognition, without visible stature.

But the Shifu understands that authority is not possession.
It is stewardship — something carried carefully, lightly, without clenching.

Shaolin discipline teaches that the hand must be firm but not rigid.
The grip must be strong enough to hold, flexible enough to release.
Strength without hardness.
Presence without grasping.

So it is with power.

The master carries authority not as a crown,
but as a responsibility.
He does not cling to it.
He does not decorate himself with it.
He holds it lightly, as one holds a vessel filled to the brim —
careful with every step, every movement, knowing that imbalance
spills what was meant to be preserved.

Power held lightly is power carried without fear.
It is not protected by arrogance or by force.
It is protected by humility, by clarity, by discipline.

The river flows through valleys, shaping them over time, not by
force, but by persistence —
never clenching the land, never grasping for recognition, simply
moving, steady, patient, enduring.

The Shifu carries power the same way.

He does not need to remind others of his authority.
He does not need to defend it with noise.
His presence is his power —
quiet, steady, real.

The undisciplined spirit believes that to loosen the grip is to lose
control.
But the master knows that clinging leads to collapse —
in the hand,
in the mind,
in the work.

To hold power lightly is to allow it to move as it must,
to trust it to endure not because it is chained,
but because it is carried with care.

The master breathes with power,
not through domination,
but through stewardship.

Authority is not a trophy to display.
It is a weight to carry —
with strength,
with humility,
with lightness.

Power, when held lightly, endures longer than power grasped with
desperation.

The Shifu steps carefully.
He moves deliberately.
He carries power not as proof of his self,
but as proof of his discipline.

And when the time comes,
he releases it —
without collapse,
without fear,
without regret.

Leading Without Chains

Leadership is not a bond that holds others captive.
It is a path walked without chains.

The undisciplined spirit mistakes leadership for control.
It seeks to bind others to itself — through loyalty demanded,
through dependence cultivated, through fear disguised as respect.

But the Shifu knows that real leadership cannot be chained.
It must be walked freely —
by the leader,
and by those who choose to follow.

Shaolin discipline teaches that the teacher's role is not to create
dependency but to cultivate independence.
The student must be strengthened, not bound.
The form must be learned, but then released — so that it can be
lived, not just repeated.

So it is with leadership.

The master does not gather followers to serve himself.
He builds them to serve the work, the path, the breath that endures
beyond any one leader.

Leading without chains means letting go of the need to be needed.
It means trusting those you guide to walk their own way, even if
they move beyond you.
It means teaching so thoroughly that your presence becomes
unnecessary.

The river does not demand that the valleys it nourishes remain
forever in its debt.
It flows, it nourishes, it moves on.

The Shifu leads the same way —
freely, carefully, without binding, without ownership.

The undisciplined mind fears loss of control.
It believes that only through holding tight can influence be

maintained.
But the master knows that control gained through fear is fragile,
while influence earned through respect endures even in absence.

Leadership without chains demands trust.
Trust in the discipline built,
trust in the breath carried forward,
trust in the endurance of those who have walked beside you.

To lead without chains is to offer guidance without ownership,
to model strength without domination,
to teach presence without demanding loyalty.

The master breathes freely —
and so invites others to breathe freely.

He does not build walls around his leadership.
He builds gates — wide enough for others to enter,
wide enough for others to leave.

Leadership is not proven by how many stay near.
It is proven by how many walk strong after the leader steps away.

The Shifu leads carefully,
without chains,
without fear,
without clinging.

And in doing so,
he teaches others to lead —
not by holding,
but by releasing.

Serving the Work, Not the Self

The highest authority is not authority over others.
It is service to the work itself.

The undisciplined spirit uses leadership to magnify the self.
It gathers power to affirm its importance, to extend its reach, to
secure its name against time.
It imagines that the work exists to serve its creator.

But the Shifu knows otherwise.

The work is not a mirror for the ego.
It is a living thing — larger than the leader, older than the self,
enduring beyond any single name or hand.

Shaolin discipline teaches that the form belongs not to the
student, not to the master, but to the way itself.
It must be practiced faithfully, offered carefully, protected without
possession.

So too must the work be served.

The master does not bend the work to fit his image.
He bends himself to fit the demands of the work —
its clarity, its endurance, its presence.

To serve the work is to build without inscribing your name on
every stone.
It is to teach without craving disciples.
It is to lead without chaining others to your shadow.

The river nourishes the land without claiming it.
The wind moves the clouds without owning the sky.

The Shifu serves the work in the same way —
invisible, necessary, steady.

The undisciplined mind seeks ownership because it fears
insignificance.
It believes that without claiming the work, the self will be
forgotten.

But the master trusts that what matters is not that the self be
remembered,
but that the work endures.

To serve the work is to disappear into it —
to carry it carefully, breathe life into it, protect it from corrosion
— and then to let it stand without needing to be seen standing
beside it.

Leadership is not self-expression.
It is self-erasure — not in the sense of vanishing, but in the sense
of stepping aside, allowing the work to be larger than the hands
that built it.

The Shifu carries the work,
but he does not brand it.
He serves it — faithfully,
quietly,
without ownership.

And when the time comes,
he releases it —
unclinging,
unclaimed,
alive.

Stillness in service.
Presence without possession.

Authority without ownership.

Chapter 27:

Victory Without Vanity

Success as Distraction

Success is not an end.
It is a temptation.

The undisciplined mind treats success as final proof — of worth,
of mastery, of arrival.
It believes that to succeed is to be completed, that to be
acknowledged is to be justified.

But the Shifu knows that success is a test —
more dangerous than failure,
more subtle than defeat.

Shaolin discipline teaches that mastery is not the moment when
applause is given.
It is the moment when the practitioner continues without needing
it.

Victory is not the enemy.
But vanity is.

Success, if not carried carefully, becomes a distraction —
pulling the mind away from the breath,
the heart away from the work,

the spirit away from the discipline that made success possible in the first place.

The river reaches the plain, expands, slows —
but it does not stop.
It does not congratulate itself.
It flows on, patient, enduring, unchanged at the root.

The Shifu moves the same way.

He does not cling to victories.
He does not decorate himself with them.
He allows them to pass through his hands,
acknowledged, but not grasped.

The undisciplined spirit wants to live in the echo of its triumphs
—
to be seen, to be praised, to be remembered.

But the master knows that such living is a slow death —
the breath shortening, the presence hollowing, the work losing its weight.

Success must not distract.
It must not be allowed to shift the mind's focus from breath to reputation,
from movement to memory,
from discipline to display.

The Shifu accepts success as he accepts failure —
without collapse,
without vanity,
without surrendering the way.

He does not deny it.
He does not belittle it.
But he does not live inside it.

The breath must continue.
The work must continue.

Victory is not a resting place.
It is only a marker passed along the endless way.

The master steps past it —
steady,
present,
unclaimed.

Success, if it distracts, will undo all that discipline has built.

But success, carried carefully,
can become another breath —
drawn fully,
released freely,
without vanity.

Gratitude Without Noise

Gratitude does not require an audience.
It does not need to be performed to be real.

The undisciplined spirit treats gratitude as spectacle —
a speech, a posture, a visible act designed not to give thanks but

to be seen giving thanks.
It mistakes noise for sincerity, display for depth.

But the Shifu knows that real gratitude is quiet.
It lives in the breath, in the stance, in the unspoken
acknowledgment of what has been given and what has been
endured.

Shaolin practice teaches that thanks are not owed to fortune, but
to discipline —
to the breath that continued,
to the body that endured,
to the unseen hours of repetition and strain.

The master feels gratitude not only for the victories,
but for the hardships,
for the failures,
for the doubt that shaped endurance.

His gratitude is not shouted.
It is carried —
in the way he continues to practice,
in the way he continues to move without clinging,
in the way he steps carefully, respectfully, fully present to the path
that has carried him forward.

Gratitude without noise is gratitude alive.

It is not words spoken to be heard.
It is breath drawn with awareness.
It is movement made with care.
It is presence sharpened by humility.

The river does not announce its thanks to the mountains it has
crossed.
It flows onward, carrying the shape of the land within it,

changed by what it has passed through,
grateful without speech.

The Shifu moves the same way.

He carries gratitude —
not as decoration,
but as discipline.

The undisciplined spirit uses gratitude as a shield for pride,
a softer mask for vanity.
But real gratitude does not seek to be seen.
It seeks only to remain present.

The master does not perform gratitude.
He lives it.

In the quiet return to breath.
In the careful continuation of the work.
In the refusal to claim victory as his own.

Gratitude without noise is the mark of the one who knows that
every success rests on unseen hands —
teachers, adversaries, failures, unseen forces.

It is the breath drawn not in triumph,
but in reverence.

The Shifu thanks the path —
not with speeches,
not with proclamations,
but with the silent continuation of his breath.

Victory without vanity.
Gratitude without noise.

Stillness — even in success.

The Invisible Triumph

The highest triumph is the one that leaves no trace.

The undisciplined mind seeks visible proof of victory —
the monument, the title, the legacy carved into stone.
It wants the world to know that it has conquered, that it has
prevailed.

But the Shifu understands that real triumph is not displayed.
It is carried.

Shaolin discipline teaches that the deepest victories are invisible
—

the breath held under pressure,
the endurance sustained in solitude,
the stillness preserved under strain.

The visible triumph fades.
The trophies tarnish.
The names are forgotten.

But the invisible triumph — the triumph of presence, of breath, of
quiet endurance — it remains.
Not in memory,
but in continuation.
Not in recognition,
but in discipline.

The river does not stop to celebrate when it reaches the sea.
It merges and disappears —
its journey complete,
its work absorbed,
its presence enduring in ways unseen.

The Shifu moves the same way.

He does not stand at the finish and demand acknowledgment.
He moves beyond it —
breath by breath,
step by step,
still carrying the same quiet presence that carried him through the
beginning.

The undisciplined spirit believes that triumph must be claimed to
be real.
But the master knows that the highest triumph needs no witness.

It is enough that the breath continues.
It is enough that the discipline endures.
It is enough that the path remains walked, even if no one
remembers who first stepped upon it.

Victory without vanity.
Gratitude without noise.
Triumph without trace.

This is the highest mastery.

The Shifu wins —
not by conquering others,
not by gathering accolades,
but by remaining whole,
by remaining present,
by remaining invisible.

Stillness is the true triumph.
Presence is the true legacy.
Endurance is the true victory.

And the master breathes —
quietly, carefully —
long after the noise has faded.

Chapter 28:

Endurance Without End

There Is No Final Arrival

The path has no finish line.
The breath has no final victory.

The undisciplined spirit craves arrival —
a moment when the labor ends, when the burden lifts, when
mastery is declared complete.
It imagines that the way is a race with a finish,
that endurance will one day be rewarded with rest without cost.

But the Shifu knows otherwise.

There is no arrival.
There is only continuation.

Shaolin discipline teaches that the practice does not culminate in
perfection.
There is no form so complete that it no longer demands
refinement,
no breath so full that it no longer requires drawing.

The river does not stop flowing when it reaches the sea.
It becomes the sea,
and in becoming, it continues.

So too does the Shifu understand that the path is not a place to reach,
but a way to be walked —
breath by breath,
step by step,
without end.

The undisciplined mind collapses when arrival does not come.
It grows bitter,
resentful that the reward seems endlessly deferred.

But the disciplined mind accepts that there is no summit from which to rest.
No final mastery to be claimed.
Only deeper endurance, quieter breath, greater patience.

The path does not end because you have tired of it.
It does not bend to the demands of fatigue,
nor does it shorten to accommodate hope.

The Shifu does not demand an end.
He demands only from himself the continuation of the breath,
the step,
the discipline —
even when no finish line appears on the horizon.

To endure without end is not to despair.
It is to mature.
It is to understand that the value is not in arriving,
but in continuing —
without collapse,
without bitterness,
without vanity.

Stillness is not a place reached.
It is a practice sustained.

Presence is not a state achieved.
It is a breath renewed.

The Shifu does not arrive.
He remains —
moving, breathing, enduring.

Endurance without end.

The path is not to be conquered.
It is to be walked —
fully,
quietly,
without end.

The Discipline of Endless Breath

The breath has no finish line.
It does not pause to celebrate itself.
It continues — quietly, steadily, invisibly.

The undisciplined mind treats discipline as a project to be
completed, a task to be checked off, a mountain to be climbed
once and for all.
It seeks to master the breath the way it seeks to master anything
— quickly, visibly, conclusively.

But the Shifu knows:
there is no mastery that ends the need for practice.
There is no final breath that closes the discipline.

Shaolin teaches that the forms must be practiced not until they are
perfected, but as long as breath fills the body.
Mastery is not the absence of practice.
It is the continuation of it.

The river does not grow tired of flowing.
It does not demand a new course simply because the old one has
become familiar.
It moves —
not because of novelty,
but because that is its nature.

The breath is the same.
It continues — not because it is always easy, not because it is
always joyful, but because to stop would be to cease living
altogether.

Discipline is not proven in the extraordinary.
It is proven in the endless ordinary —
the breath drawn without announcement,
the practice continued without ceremony,
the step taken without applause.

The undisciplined spirit demands progress it can measure,
milestones it can display.
But the master asks only for the breath to continue —
steady, quiet, unseen.

The discipline of endless breath is the discipline of presence
without fatigue.
It is the choice to continue even when the body is weary,

even when the mind is restless,
even when the spirit hungers for conclusion.

It is the endurance that endures —
not because it is easy,
not because it is rewarded,
but because it is the way.

The Shifu draws breath not to arrive,
but to remain.

He breathes not for victory,
but for presence.

He practices not for perfection,
but for continuation.

Stillness is not an achievement.
It is a breath.
Drawn again.
And again.
And again.

Endless breath.
Endless endurance.

The way is not finished.
The way continues.

Presence Without Destination

Presence does not require a destination.
It requires only attention.

The undisciplined mind seeks presence as a means to an end —
as a strategy for success,
as a technique for achievement,
as a way to reach some imagined final place where effort is no
longer needed.

But the Shifu knows that real presence has no destination.
It is not a bridge to somewhere else.
It is the way itself.

Shaolin discipline teaches that the form is not a step toward
mastery.
It is mastery — lived moment by moment, breath by breath,
without needing to be anything more than itself.

So too with presence.

Presence is not preparation.
It is arrival — not at a place, but in the moment.

The river does not flow to arrive somewhere better than itself.
It flows because that is its nature.
It moves not toward achievement, but in fulfillment of what it
already is.

The master understands that seeking a destination fractures the
breath.
It pulls attention forward, away from what is, toward what might

be —
imagined, desired, unattainable.

But the breath drawn fully,
the step taken carefully,
the silence carried patiently —
this is presence.

The undisciplined spirit rushes through moments in pursuit of
others.
It trades the certainty of now for the illusion of a future it cannot
grasp.

But the master remains.
Not because he is slow.
Not because he has no ambition.
But because he knows that life,
discipline,
endurance —
all of it exists only in the present.

Presence without destination is the highest endurance.
It is the refusal to chase.
It is the refusal to abandon what is real for what is imagined.

The Shifu breathes fully —
not to arrive somewhere,
but to be fully here.

He moves carefully —
not to reach an end,
but because the movement itself is the way.

Presence is the end.
It is the work.

It is the breath.
It is the discipline.

There is no beyond.
There is only now.

Endurance without end.
Breath without finish.
Presence without destination.

The master remains —
breathing,
moving,
enduring —
not toward,
but within.

Epilogue:

Return to the Gate

Full circle — the Monk and the Shifu are not separate.

The journey, though it seems long, is always a circle.

In the beginning, there was the Monk — sitting in stillness, learning endurance, gathering patience. The world was outside, distant, something to be observed but not yet entered. The Monk trained in silence, shaped himself in solitude, prepared without knowing what he was preparing for.

But solitude was not the destination.
Stillness was not the end.
It was the beginning.

The Shifu steps where the Monk once sat.
He moves where the Monk once waited.
He acts where the Monk once endured.
But he carries with him the same center — the stillness learned in the waiting, the silence learned in the listening.

The Monk and the Shifu are not separate beings.
They are the same — only at different points along the arc of becoming.

The Monk built the foundation.
The Shifu lives upon it.

The Monk learned to be still.
The Shifu learned to move without losing the stillness.

They are not stages to be graduated from, but states to be carried
— together, inseparable.
Stillness in motion.
Silence in speech.
Calm in action.

There is no true movement without stillness behind it.
No true leadership without solitude beneath it.
No real mastery without the long, quiet apprenticeship to the
invisible.

The Monk did not disappear when the Shifu arrived.
He remains — deeper, quieter, the unseen anchor beneath the
motion.

And so the journey returns to the gate — the same place it began,
but seen with different eyes.
Not as a barrier now, but as a threshold.
Not as a place of waiting, but as a place of passing through.
Not as an end, but as a beginning that never truly ends.

The circle closes.
The path continues.

The Monk and the Shifu — still, always, one.

Stillness and motion complete one life.

Stillness alone is not a life.
Motion alone is not a life.
It is only together — stillness and motion — that a life becomes whole.

Stillness without motion can become stagnation — a retreat from the world, a refusal to engage, a clinging to quiet that hardens into isolation.
Motion without stillness becomes frenzy — movement without meaning, achievement without depth, endless noise drowning out the quiet truths.

Shaolin teaches the integration.
The stance rooted in the ground, still — yet ready to move in any direction.
The breath steady, calm — yet carrying strength into every strike.
The mind silent, clear — yet awake and engaged with every moment that passes.

Stillness is not the absence of life; it is its grounding.
Motion is not the rejection of peace; it is its extension.

A life that moves from stillness carries a different weight.
Each act is deliberate.
Each word is measured.
Each movement is informed by something deeper — a quiet reservoir of clarity, a deep well of patience.

Stillness makes the motion meaningful.
Motion makes the stillness visible.

One is the breath in.
One is the breath out.
One gathers; the other releases.
Together, they form the full rhythm of living.

The Monk teaches how to be still without disappearing.
The Shifu teaches how to move without losing yourself.

To master one is not to forsake the other.
It is to weave them together — to live with a mind that knows
when to wait and when to act, a heart that knows when to hold
and when to release.

Stillness and motion are not two ways of life.
They are one — the root and the branch, the breath and the voice,
the silence and the song.

One life.
Fully lived.

Afterword

The work does not end here.

What is built must be maintained.
What is known must be re-learned.
What is silent must be honored even in motion.

There is no graduation from mastery.
Only a deeper walking.

If these pages have been a companion,
let them remain so —
but do not mistake them for the journey itself.

The journey is yours now.
Quiet. Steady. Unfolding.

The next work is yours to build.
Walk slowly. Move intentionally. Stay rooted.

There are no final words.
Only quieter steps.